Isaac Hazelhurst Esq

with the Respects of

Lindley Smith

June 12 1851

DOCUMENTS

RELATING TO THE

MANUFACTURE OF IRON

IN PENNSYLVANIA.

Published on behalf of the Convention of Iron Masters,

WHICH MET IN PHILADELPHIA, ON THE TWENTIETH OF DECEMBER, 1849.

See Table of Contents, at page 113.

PHILADELPHIA:
PUBLISHED BY THE GENERAL COMMITTEE.
1850.

MEMORIAL.

TO THE SENATE AND HOUSE OF REPRESENTATIVES OF THE UNITED STATES OF AMERICA IN CONGRESS ASSEMBLED:

YOUR Memorialists, interested in the manufacture of iron in the State of Pennsylvania, ask leave to offer some considerations and statements suggested by the suffering condition of that industry. We are not unaware of the prejudice which exists in the minds of many, against the propriety of the government giving any attention to the grievances of manufacturers; neither are we ignorant of the grounds of this feeling.

It is a part of our purpose in this memorial, to lessen, if we cannot wholly remove this prejudice. On a subject of such importance, involving so many interests, in a country so extended as ours, it is to be expected that honest differences of opinion will exist, and sectional, if not clashing, claims will arise. The manufacturers of this country, whatever may be their troubles, must yield with all their fellow-citizens to that system of compromise on which all our institutions are adjusted. We cannot ask any legislation for our advantage unless it be, if not equally for the benefit, at least not injurious to the rest of the community. On this ground we are willing to base our present application for relief. We come, without distinction of party, and ask to be heard upon strictly national considerations, that if any enactment is consequent upon our petition, it may be regarded as permanent and not partial legislation. We ask not for relief to-day which may be withdrawn to-morrow; but, for a settled policy. We ask to have the wisdom of all interests and all parties applied to the preparation of such a system as will be permitted to stand, subject only to the improvements which experience and time may dictate.

It cannot be questioned, that a large supply of iron is necessary to the rapid progress of any country in all departments of industry and the arts, in civilization and the material well-being of the people. The production of iron in Great Britain is equal to that of all Europe beside; while her consumption is equal to a million and a third of tons, or about 100 lbs. to each individual of the whole population. Belgium falls little, if any, short of an equal consumption for each inhabitant. Sweden would stand next in order but that she exports so much of her iron as to remain far behind Belgium in proportionate consumption. France consumes about 30 lbs. for each person, and of this, about one-tenth is imported. The rest of Europe does not consume 10 lbs. each person, and the remainder of the old world does not reach a consumption of 5 lbs. In this respect the enterprise and industry of the people of the United States have not permitted them to remain behind; so that despite of obstacles the most formidable and the most vacillating legislation, we stand in the front rank of nations as to the consumption of iron. Our consumption is equal to that of Great Britain for each inhabitant; but we import about two-tenths of the quantity consumed. Such is the abundance of raw materials, such the enterprise of our people, such the tendency to employ iron, and so greatly are the facilities for transportation multiplying, that we might with certainty outstrip the world in its production. All that is needed to secure such a result is a steady home market. Pennsylvania now produces as much iron as Great Britain did in 1820; her product has doubled in ten years, under great disadvantages, and in ten years of favouring legislation, it might be doubled again. Pennsylvania now produces as much iron as France; more than Russia and Sweden united; and more than all Germany. Yet how many States of the Union will ere long manufacture as much as Pennsylvania, for there are few in which the raw materials do not abound. Our population is destined to increase in a very rapid ratio; under a wise policy the production of iron would far more than keep pace, until we should be finally as much distinguished for the consumption of iron as we now are for the production of cotton.

The policy of purchasing only in the cheapest market sends not only the people of the United States, but of all the Continent of Europe, and in fact of all the world, to Great Britain for iron; for there the cost of making is one half less than here, and in still greater disproportion with most other nations. The difficulty is, that the manufacturers and merchants of that country are not governed by the cost of production in selling their commodities, but by the extent and urgency of the demand. When there is a demand, the prices are at the highest; when there is not, the world is invited to a cheap market.

If it be objected to such a development of the manufacture of iron, that the cost of production is too great in the United States, and that we ought rather to import that which is purchased cheaper in other countries; the reply may be made that, Great Britain being the only country, in which iron is sold at lower rates than here, our demand could only go to that market; that if sound economy requires us to obtain our supply of iron in Great Britain, the same motive would send all other nations to the same market. But our orders alone could not be filled without so raising the price, as to preclude all possibility of our obtaining a full supply. If we should order from Great Britain in one year, additionally, half the quantity of iron we now manufacture, prices would go higher than they have been for a century, in England or America. The British iron market is cheap when you refrain from it, not when you press upon it. The cost of manufacturing iron is far from being the only, or even the chief controlling element of the price. The manufacturers and holders of iron in Great Britain are extremely sensitive to a demand for any increased quantity of iron or to any increased urgency of demand, whether from abroad or for home consumption.

A million of tons of iron, which is the amount of our consumption when the industry of the country is suffering under no depressing causes, would have cost in Great Britain, in 1843, at the prices then prevailing, (taking half the amount as pig and half as bar iron,) £3,500,000 sterling. In 1846, the same quantity would have cost £9,000,000 sterling, at which price it was more economical to manufacture than to import. These high prices gave an immense impulse to the production of this country, and showed how promptly capital and enterprise combined to overcome an emergency by which the country was threatened with a deficiency of the indispensable article of iron.

Had we even a stipulation, by treaty, on the part of the government of Great Britain, that we should always be furnished with iron in that market at the low rates now current, say a million of tons for $20,000,000, how could we pay for it? We already import more than we can pay for in exports.

All the shrewdness and enterprise of our merchants are constantly at work to increase our exports; not only is everything exported that will pay a profit, but every article that will pay a freight. How absurd to suppose we could pay $20,000,000 additional for iron. Any attempt to supply ourselves with iron from abroad would, if persevered in, reduce our consumption from 100 lbs. for each person to far less than half that quantity, besides abridging our imports of other articles, and wholly deranging our foreign commerce.

As manufacturers of iron, we freely admit that we enjoy in Pennsylvania, and, we may add, in all the United States, very manifold natural advantages. If we could now boast that exemption from injurious rivalry, enjoyed by the British manufacturers, during the rapid growth of their industry, we could safely promise even greater results than have been witnessed elsewhere. Look for a moment at the circumstances under which the British manufacture of iron was developed. There was no surplus of pig iron in any country of Europe, and the article was unknown in European foreign commerce. All that England ever imported was a few thousand tons from the colonies of Pennsylvania, Maryland, and Virginia, and this was finally cut off by our revolution. The English manufacturer of pig iron had no rival, and required no protection. The only competitors in bar iron were Russia and Sweden; their prices, from 1780 to 1849, ranged from £12 to £25 per ton. But as if this high price was not ample protection to British manufacturers, the government advanced the duties fifteen times between 1780 and 1820 without one reduction, increasing them from £2 10 to £7 per ton, affording the double protection of high prices and constantly increasing duties.

Between 1780 and 1825 Russian and Swedish bars could not be imported and sold in England for less than £20 or $100 the ton; this gave the English manufacturers entire possession of the home market for all purposes to which their iron was applicable, and yet their price was always below the foreign.

In contrast with this, the American maker of bar iron competes with rivals whose average home price is only £8 or $40 the ton, and who, at present rates of iron in the British markets, and duties here, can put their bars in our market at $40, duty paid. It is true, they lose money by the operation, but they would lose more by selling at home and thus further depressing the markets in which they must sell three times as much as they export. Thus they preserve their own, and ruin the markets of their competitors. During the rise of this manufacture in Great Britain pig iron was worth in their market over 100 shillings, generally 120 shillings. The American manufacturer encounters pig iron sold in Scotland for years together at from 35 to 45 shillings, and which can now be put down in our markets, duty paid, at 60 to 70 shillings.

If we ask relief against such ruinous competition, we derive countenance from the fact, that British manufacturers constantly appealed to their government for protection under the favourable circumstances we have noted. We have seen with what success. The time was not long until in 1825, the manufacture having attained ample growth and power, it could dispense with all aid, and defy competition. Great

Britain had then risen to the rank of the largest consumer of iron in the world.

If this business has been overdone in Great Britain the evil consequences have fallen upon the manufacturers. The public has enjoyed an immense advantage in the abundance of a material so important in every department of industry as iron. The fluctuations in price which have ensued from this large production have been of late years so great as to cast in the shade all other commercial changes of price. The range of these fluctuations in pig iron during the last ten years is from £1 18s. to £5 12s. 6d. and in bar iron £4 10s. to £13, or about 200 per cent.

In one extremity of this fluctuation, British iron becomes too high to import under a revenue duty; in the other too low to admit of home production. In the one extreme we cannot afford to use it; in the other, it paralyses our efforts to manufacture for ourselves.

The legislation asked by American manufacturers deserves not the odium so frequently heaped upon it. We know that we can furnish to the consumers of this country a million of tons of iron cheaper and better than it can be had abroad. We ask for defence against those commercial fluctuations which occur in Great Britain, from causes wholly originating there, and which, while they thrust down the prices of iron there far below the cost of making, throw large and irregular quantities into our ports, disturbing the regular course of industry here; breaking down our markets and carrying ruin, at each such invasion, into many establishments. If we ask aid against such irregularities, it is no more than we should be obliged to do, if the manufacture in the United States, were as greatly developed as in Great Britain, and enjoying, in all respects, equal advantages. If that were the case, each of the equally powerful competitors, would seek to relieve their home markets in seasons of depression, by thrusting the rejected surplus upon his rival; and each would seize the opportunity of high prices in the other to make large exports, until both markets, unable to maintain any high prices to compensate for unfavourable periods, would sink into hopeless depression and the business perish or be greatly impaired. Against such consequences both would appeal to their respective governments for protection, not for monopoly; for that security against ruinous fluctuations, and that regularity in sales, indispensable to the success of industry. Competitors at home can observe their mutual progress, and take their measures of defence in time, but that competition which comes from abroad, cannot be watched, nor preparation made for its sudden inroads. If the British manufacturer is prevented from flooding our markets at less than the average upon which his business thrives, a mere revenue duty will be ample protection against the great advantage he enjoys, of employing labour at less than half the cost paid in the United States.

Among those most deeply interested in the vigour and prosperity of our iron manufactures are the farmers who furnish food, and the planters and manufacturers who furnish clothing, for our operatives in iron. We cannot here fully unfold the chain of mutual interests which binds all branches of industry together, nor exhibit its strength, and the importance of preserving it unbroken. We ask attention to only a few prominent facts. When the ports of Great Britain were opened to our agricultural products, it was fondly hoped that our farmers would find there an unlimited market for wheat and maize. At the present moment, however, these are very little higher in Liverpool than in Philadelphia, and the pressure of any increased export would sink prices there below ours. At the present rates of iron and flour in Liverpool, the flour made from an acre of good wheat will about exchange for a ton of pig iron, and pay for its transportation to this country. If we take the product of the acre at four barrels, worth now in our market $18 or $20, it will exchange here for a ton of pig iron of far superior quality.

But farmers who feed the manufacturers of iron in the United States do much better than exchanging the product of an acre for a ton of pig iron. A furnace yielding 4,000 tons of pig iron gives employment to two hundred labourers, each of whom consumes annually fifty dollars worth of food. Of this but one-tenth is expended for bread; the remainder is consumed in the shape of mutton, veal, pork, beef, poultry, potatoes, turnips, beets, and other products of garden, field, and orchard; the production of which in great variety is an accompaniment of all good husbandry and profitable farming. To import 100 tons of pig iron requires the product of 100 acres of wheat; but in our home markets the usual product of 50 acres will exchange for 100 tons of pig iron. An acre of potatoes, the cultivation of which does not exceed in expense that of Indian corn, will exchange for eight tons of pig iron in the markets of Philadelphia. The farmer who, with 100 acres of wheat, prefers the foreign market, will receive for his crop 100 tons of pig iron, at present rates worth $2,000, whilst he who has a hundred acres of potatoes can exchange his crop at home for 800 tons of iron, worth $16,000.

Wheat sent to a distant market, which fluctuates according to the supply and demand, must be sold without reference to the cost of production, and without control of the producer for what it will bring in competition with all the world. What the farmer sells at home is at his own price, and is sold or held according to his discretion. Well-cultivated lands dependent on a foreign market may be worth from $5 to $20 per acre; those that have the full advantage of a home market are worth from $50 to $200. If the production of iron in Pennsylvania were continued in full activity for ten years, it would double the value of her own lands and make a vast contribution to the value of other lands and property beyond her boundaries.

What is applicable to the propriety of sending wheat to a distant market to be exchanged for iron, is just as true applied to the expediency of sending raw cotton to England, to be exchanged for manufactured cotton, or any other foreign goods. The cotton plantations can feed the operatives necessary to manufacture all their cotton; and such a policy would triple the value of every cotton plantation in the country. To produce this additional quantity of food would probably require no more labourers than are now employed in growing cotton. It would only require that division of labour which is as important to the success of the planter and farmer as to that of any other producer.

To manufacture 800,000 tons of iron, the present product of the United States, gives support to upwards of 250,000 persons, to whom at least twenty millions in wages must be paid. Of this sum $4,000,000 will be expended in coarse cotton fabrics for clothing and furniture, $3,000,000 for woollens, and $3,000,000 for other items of clothing and domestic comfort. The $20,000,000 earned by the operatives in iron will thus be diffused over the whole country, giving vigour and activity to numberless branches of industry. The South will furnish cotton, sugar, and rice; the Middle States bread, potatoes, and meat; and the Northern States the products of the loom; whilst thousands of tailors, hatters, shoemakers, and other tradesmen, find constant employment in ministering to the necessities of the makers of iron, consuming themselves an additional quantity of food and clothing by a demand distributed in like manner.

It is said the domestic cost of manufacturing iron is too high to be sustained by any sound legislation, or to warrant any large consumption. We reply that our whole supply cannot be imported as cheaply as we manufacture it; for the reason, that the cost is not the only controlling element of price, and that our large demands, if made upon the British market, would quickly enhance prices far beyond the domestic rates. We must, therefore, manufacture at home at least three-fourths of our consumption; and, to do this, our manufactures must be maintained in full vigour by remunerating prices and a steady market. Iron costs twice as much to manufacture here as in Great Britain; because employers here pay double, and more than double, for wages of labour. The labourers of the United States can be fully employed at the high wages which prevail here, and we are not prepared to say that these wages are more than a just compensation for labour. It is certain that in most countries where less rates are paid a large mass of the population is in a state of destitution, and sunk to the lowest grade of human existence. In this country, where physical well-being is so easily attainable, should we not feed, clothe and lodge, our labourers in comfort, and keep them out of the poor-house? The wages now paid are only sufficient for this, and to enable the prudent to make some savings for sickness, reverses, and old age. We are not, therefore, in favour of any system which contemplates a reduction of wages, and a consequent degradation of our working men. We believe that the consumption of every country is regulated by the wages of the labourer: if he is liberally paid he will consume freely. The mass of the consumers in a country must be the labourers; and, when these are able to exact a fair compensation for their toil, all prices must soon be adjusted upon the same scale. The manufacturer will demand for his product a price proportioned to the cost of labour; the farmer must do the same, and so on through the whole circle of industry. The labourer himself contributes to sustain these prices by a consumption proportioned to his income. All persons concerned in this adjustment being in a condition to ask and obtain justice, the whole system of consumption will be regulated by the rights of all and the means of all. In this state of things the largest possible consumption can take place; because it will be the result of a fair exchange. The stimulus to exertion and increased production will be complete, because every product of industry can be exchanged, at a fair rate, for other products. If no disturbing cause intervenes, the production and consumption need have no other limit than the physical ability of the producing parties and their mutual wants.

In full activity of business in the United States, our consumption of iron has reached 100 lbs. for each person. If no disturbing cause had interfered, we should now be consuming 200 lbs. Our farmers could amply feed the labourers needful to such an increased production, and our machinists and mechanics could soon, under the operation of such a system, work up and prepare it for consumption. Every branch of industry would have all the rest for customers; and, if all measured their values by the same scale, all would be rewarded according to their industry. It is well known that low prices of iron are no boon to those who buy to work up and sell, and that the seasons of highest prices are often periods of largest consumption. In 1847 pig iron ranged above 30 dollars per ton in this country, yet at these high prices the whole stock of that year, estimated at 750,000 tons, was consumed; all the old stocks and remnants were swept off, and it was perfectly apparent, to those well acquainted with the state of the market, that there was an actual deficiency of supply to the extent of very nearly, if not quite 100,000 tons. In 1849, with pig iron at 20 dollars and bar iron at 50 dollars, the consumption of the country has probably fallen off one-third, and the production one-half. With this diminished production domestic stocks are now accumulating rapidly. Of the amount imported this year a very large proportion yet remains in the market. The quantity of iron now on hand in this country is estimated at 300,000 tons; and of this one-half is British. The manufacturers of castings, of machinery and hardware, now find that the consumption of their articles is checked, and that the low price of their raw material is not only no benefit, but a positive evil, and they are ready, equally with the makers of iron, to ask for a remedy. A similar result will be found by comparing all the periods of high and low prices.

To whom, then, enures the advantages of cheap foreign iron? Abundance of food is no more beneficial to a man in the agonies of a fatal disorder, than cheap iron to a paralysed industry. The ability of the country to consume iron depends on the vigour and activity of all departments of industry. If agriculture languishes, the consumption of iron is diminished; if the machinery of the north is idle, or partially so, the demand for iron falls off, and so if cotton or sugar are selling at inadequate rates.

At the present moment various interests are suffering from the utter stagnation of the iron trade, as the operatives in iron will this year, 1849, consume in supply of their wants some twelve millions of dollars less than in 1847. This alone is enough to carry serious injury into numberless channels of industry. It especially affects the consumption of cottons and woollens; for the use of these can be abridged to a greater extent than food. All interests are, therefore, bound together by common ties; when one suffers all suffer. It is a great mistake to suppose that the producers of cotton, sugar, rice, and tobacco, have no special interest in the activity of manufacturing industry in the other States. A very large proportion of the cotton crop is now consumed in the United States, and thus kept from the British market, already so liberally supplied as to give British merchants control of the price. When British iron is exported to us for want of a market at home, we take it at our own price; when we order large quantities of iron we pay what they can exact. Our cotton is mainly exported, disgorged upon the British market, and the price is made in Liverpool. When British manufacturers shall be compelled to come hither for their cotton, the price will be made by the planters. The present supply is so large, that the price is yearly the result of mere speculation. What is sold in this country is clear gain to the planter, as the whole crop would sell for no more in Great Britain than the quantity which now goes there. If half the crop was consumed at home the other half would sell for as much in Great Britain as is realized for the quantity now exported. This result is not only attainable under favouring legislation—but it might have been attained before now, by that wise policy which stimulates home industry to its utmost capacities. By such a policy the consumption of cotton and iron could be doubled in a few years, with immense advantage to the wealth and happiness of our whole population. It is the interest of the planter not to struggle for that division of labour among nations; which makes one nation a planter of cotton, another of sugar, another a maker of iron, another a spinner, another a weaver, another a tailor, and so on: but that division of labour which mingles these pursuits in the same country, in the same county, in the same town, and, to some extent, on the same plantation. This is the division of labour which begets a vast production and consumption at home, and an internal trade with which no foreign commerce can ever vie.

Who can doubt, that if the planting States were legislating for themselves, their first care would not be to become more independent, to diversify their labour and vary its products? What such legislation would compel them to do, they can now do under that national legislation which is invoked by others. They are already entering upon that career—it will be found not only the sure road to prosperity for them, but also for us. We so fully confide in the doctrine of the division of labour at home, that we not only trust the cotton planters will manufacture as much of their cotton at home as they can, and feed the operatives thus employed, but also manufacture as much of their iron as they can. There is room for all, work for all, and market at home for such a large portion of our products that the remainder will not overcharge the channels of foreign commerce and be sacrificed for the advantage of foreign merchants and manufacturers.

We object to the doctrine that industrial pursuits are subordinate to foreign commerce; and that the latter is to be considered as the rightful patron of industry. In our view, industry stands first in natural order, and should be the first care of the legislator. Commerce is merely an agency, the charges of which, as well as its powers, should be kept to the lowest point consistent with efficiency. It may suit those engaged in commerce to insist upon the "Let us alone" policy, for, doubtless, merchants can take care of themselves, and thrive not the less, when the producers, from whom their profits come, are suffering most. The manufacturer has, in all countries, asked for special legislation, and under its good effects, the present manufacturing systems of Europe and this country have grown to their present magnitude. The relative importance of the domestic production of this country and its foreign commerce, may be seen in the fact that our foreign commerce yields from six to eight dollars' worth of foreign commodities to the consumption of each individual of our population; whilst the domestic industry of the country furnishes not less than from 75 to 100 dollars for each person. Shall we pursue a policy impairing the power that produces the larger supply, in the vain attempt to add the worth of a dollar or two a head, to the quantity of foreign commodities consumed? And be it noted, that every dollar a head added to our consumption of foreign goods adds over 21,000,000 dollars to our imports.

If an ample supply of iron be indispensable to national progress and national welfare, and if the whole of that supply cannot be imported as cheaply as it can be made at home, the principle which should govern legislation applied to this industry, and to others in like circumstances, is clearly discernible. If home production, on which we rely for more than three-fourths of our consumption, is not sustained in that activity which insures its proceeding with economy and advantage, it must flag; and the product being diminished, a greater demand must be thrown upon the foreign market, enhancing the prices of importation. But if the home production is adequately sustained by a free market, it can supply all the channels of consumption. Legislation, marking closely the line of vigorous production at home, will encourage importation, with the double purpose of obtaining revenue, and keeping the manufacturers at home to fair prices.

Sustain the domestic manufacturer at the point of full production, and then admit the foreign article freely. The more closely our revenue enactments approximate this object, the more perfectly will they encourage domestic industry, obtain the largest attainable revenue, and best secure the interests of consumers. The manufacturer, constantly struggling to keep up his prices, will be as constantly met by foreign iron, selling at such rates as to keep him to the line of public advantage. It is the operation of a well-managed competition between the domestic and foreign producer, which results in the greatest benefit to the consumer. If the consumer is driven to a foreign market for his supplies, or for too large a proportion of them, prices will be inordinately advanced against him; while, if the foreign market is prohibited, or too heavily burdened, the same undue advance may take place at home. But if foreign iron is introduced at the point designated, it not only works no injury, but produces positive public good, as to revenue and prices, and also as to the increased consumption of iron. There are certain average rates at which manufacturers of iron in this country can live and flourish, and these rates are very little, if any, above those to which the often recurring fluctuations of prices in Great Britain are carried. At these rates, which are easily ascertained by the legislator, the line of competition can be established, with the greatest advantage to the consumer. They will not exclude foreign iron, but frequently attract it. During the last fiscal year, the very large importation of 315,000 tons of iron has taken place. Of this, much the larger proportion has probably been sent to us on foreign account, because there was no demand at home; it was sent to save the home market, already broken down, from further depression. It has broken down our markets; and, if sold at present rates, will not yield the makers a penny of profit. This iron, coming thus to a bad market, came because it would have been worse for the holders to keep it at home. If previous legislation had shielded our market, so as to maintain prices remunerating to our manufacturers, the additional duty necessary for this purpose would not have deterred the export of iron to this country; for, while those who shipped it to our ports must have paid a higher duty, they would have realized better prices. A ton of iron rails, under the present tariff, at the prices prevailing in 1846 and 1847, was charged with a duty of twenty dollars, which was almost prohibitory, and therefore produced little revenue, making foreign rails cost 90 dollars per ton. During the year 1849, a ton of rails has been charged with only eight dollars, and has, of course, produced but little revenue; whilst a ton of rails were laid down in our market at 45 dollars, injuring the domestic producer to an extent that is incalculable. A system of revenue which would meet the low prices by a proportionate increase of duty, and make provision for high rates by a like reduction, never excluding the foreign iron, would, we believe, meet the exigencies of domestic industry, and greatly increase the revenue. Whatever may be the advantages of the *ad valorem* system in other cases, they are more than neutralized by the fluctuations of the prices of British iron. It is true that a part of this objection applies with equal force to specific duties; for, when these are high enough to meet the difficulty of low prices, they become prohibitory when prices rise. These considerations furnish a strong inducement for special provisions in our revenue system in regard to foreign iron. A system could thus be devised which would give a mighty impetus to the production and consumption of iron, and to other dependent branches of industry. A home competition could be thus insured, which would, in the end, reduce the price of iron to the lowest limits consistent with undiminished production. Under such a policy, we should soon surpass Great Britain in the quantity of iron made and consumed, as much as we do now in the quality. We should employ hosts of labourers, and attract them hither from all quarters of the world; and for every million of people which this scene of industry would draw to our shores, we should be furnished with an additional home market, equivalent in amount, and far more remunerative, than the average export of our foreign trade.

In closing this memorial, we ask your intervention in our favour, and the insertion of such provisions in our revenue laws as will "regulate commerce with foreign nations" in iron, and exclude from our markets the results of those destructive fluctuations and irregularities which originate in foreign causes, and should expend their force on foreign shores. This being done, we only ask further that such duties be imposed upon foreign iron as will bring the largest revenue to the public treasury.

CIRCULAR.

SIR:

The undersigned* MANUFACTURERS AND DEALERS IN IRON, beg leave to invite your co-operation in a Meeting of parties interested in the business, to be held in this City, on Thursday, 20th instant, at 10 A. M. They hope they may rely on your aid. You are doubtless aware, measures tending to relieve the Iron interest from its present extreme depression, by enforcing upon Congress the necessity of a revision of the Tariff, have been in progress during the present summer; the necessity of such a change has, we think, become apparent to the moderate men of all parties, and we have reason to hope, that with proper efforts on the part of the friends of the measure, the most gratifying success awaits the movement.

The object of the proposed meeting is to insure this result; and it is of such vital importance to us all, that we venture to express the hope, that no ordinary obstacle will be permitted to prevent your meeting us at the time named.

We take occasion to say, that we wish to avoid entirely all connexion with party politics; we propose to meet as business men only, and as such to appeal to Congress, without distinction of party, for the preservation of a great American interest. We believe the time has now come when the question can be withdrawn from the contests of party, and adjusted on a permanent and satisfactory footing.

Reeves, Buck, & Co.
Colwell & Co.
Coleman, Kelton & Campbell.
Jos. & Geo. P. Whitaker.
Fisher, Morgan & Co.
Bevan & Humphreys.
M. B. Buckley & Son.

Philadelphia, December 6th, 1849.

Pursuant to the foregoing notice, the Convention assembled on Thursday, December 20th, in the Chamber of the Board of Trade, and was organized by appointing

THOMAS CHAMBERS,
Of Montour Iron Works,
Chairman.

Charles E. Smith,
Nathan Rowland,
Secretaries.

The following Committees were appointed:

On a Memorial—

Stephen Colwell,
George P. Whitaker.
Robert Kelton,

On Resolutions—

Lindley Fisher,
M. Brooke Buckley,
A. S. Hewett,
James T. Hodge.

On the State of the Trade and Statistics—

Charles E. Smith,
P. B. Savery,
Abraham S. Valentine.

On Finance—

Robert Coleman,
Lindley Fisher.
Samuel J. Reeves,

On the Operation of the Ad Valorem Principle as a Revenue Measure—

SAMUEL J. REEVES, FREDERICK OVERMAN.
H. HALDEMAN.

Messrs. Colwell, Smith, Reeves, and Coleman presented Reports from their respective Committees, which were read and adopted.

Mr. Fisher, from the Committee on Resolutions, presented the following RESOLUTIONS, which were read twice and passed separately :—

1. Resolved, That a crisis has arisen in the iron business which calls for the immediate revision of the revenue laws, so far as that article is concerned, and that the number of establishments which have already been forced to suspend by the influx of foreign iron, proves that without such a change, the business cannot permanently sustain itself in its rightful position, as a great branch of our national industry.

2. Resolved, That the manufacture of iron is not a mere local or individual interest, but is of national importance, as affording a supply of a chief element of progress in time of peace, and an important engine of defence in time of war.

3. Resolved, That it has been the policy of every civilized government to extend a fostering care to the production of iron; and that the example of Great Britain is especially worthy of notice, who, by an unwavering course of favouring legislation, sustained the business in its infancy, when its prospects, without that aid, were far less encouraging than they now are in this country, and never removed its protecting care, until it reached a development unparalleled in the history of trade; by which the consumer is supplied at the lowest rates, and the manufacturer defies the competition of the world.

4. Resolved, That in this country the development of its industry and of its various natural resources has been so rapid during the last few years, that the only remaining serious impediments to the establishment of the iron business here on a firm basis, lie in the high price of labour in this country compared with that which rules in foreign countries with which we compete, and in the enormous fluctuations which have prevailed in the price of iron.

5. Resolved, That experience teaches that the difficulties produced

by these causes cannot, in the present state of the trade, be overcome by any unassisted efforts on the part of the manufacturers; that the business is now prostrated and wide-spread ruin threatened because they are exposed to them, and that an efficient remedy is only to be found in the action of the General Government.

6. Resolved, That in raising revenue by duties on imports, the Government can readily apply this remedy, by imposing such a rate of duty as shall establish *a fair competition* with the foreign article, and without *prohibiting* its introduction, build up such a domestic production as shall always keep the price of foreign iron in check; and that it is the manifest interest of the *consumer of iron*, who must in any event be taxed for revenue, to have this tax so framed, if possible, as to prevent the foreign maker from obtaining control of the market and fixing his own price, as he may do in the absence of domestic production.

7. Resolved, That the present ad valorem duty on iron might, as suggested by the late Secretary of the Treasury, be increased with advantage to the revenue, but that the ad valorem system cannot possibly meet the true and mutual interest of consumer and producer, because the fluctuations in price are aggravated, instead of being relieved, by duties which increase as the price rises, and diminish as the price falls; thus subjecting the consumer, on the one hand to supply his wants at extravagant rates, and the producer, on the other, to a hopeless struggle against the cheap labour of Europe, combined with the immense capital accumulated in years of high prices at the expense of the unprotected consumer.

8. Resolved, That the ad valorem system, moreover, operates precisely as if a new tariff were enacted at every change of price; that it encourages frauds upon the revenue, because a small invoice price produces a duty proportionably low; that it tends to throw the importing business of the country into dishonest hands; that it offers a virtual bonus upon the consumption of inferior articles, and this operates to degrade the national taste, and retard the onward march of improvement, while, at the same time, its practical operation has not developed a single advantage which the "specific" system does not also possess.

9. Resolved, That specific duties, on the other hand, tend to counteract the fluctuations of trade, and insure regularity to the business of the country, as the producer can then calculate with comparative certainty upon the competition against which he has to contend, and can

establish his production upon so firm a basis, that on the average of years as cheap, if not cheaper prices, are insured to the consumer.

10. Resolved, That the true test of national prosperity is to be found in the price of labour, which can only be maintained at a permanently high rate by opening every possible avenue of employment to receive the ever-increasing supply; that the ad valorem system of duties tend to narrow the field of labour, and consequently to reduce its reward.

11. Resolved, That the employment of labour in manufactures, by diverting a large amount from agriculture, insures a home market and better prices to the farmer.

12. Resolved, That the cotton planter is equally interested with the farmer in securing large wages and diversified employment to labour, because it increases the ability of the community to consume, thus securing at the same time a large home market for cotton, and by reducing the quantity forced upon the foreign market, a higher price for that staple.

13. Resolved, Therefore, That the *protection* which this Convention desires, is protection for the *Government* against frauds upon the revenue; for the *importer* against dishonest competition; for the *producer* against the unnatural fluctuations of trade; for the *consumer* against high prices of iron, which are rendered inevitable by the absence of domestic production; for the *labourer* against the meagre rewards which a narrower field for employment must occasion; and for the *farmer* and *planter* against the obvious disadvantages of a single market, and the loss of intrinsic value entailed upon his produce by the expense of transporting it abroad.

14. Resolved, Therefore, That it is the sense of this Convention, that stability and permanence in the tariff law, is the first and most essential requisite to a healthy state of the Iron trade, and that, as manufacturers, we prefer the lowest duty that will enable us to prosecute our business, provided it be permanent, to a higher one with a prospect of a change in a few years, and that we are indifferent whether this object is effected by the imposition of specific duties, or the adoption of a sliding scale, so framed as to counteract the fluctuations in price.

15. Resolved, That this meeting expressly disclaims all political

motives, and all desire to further the views of any party by its action; that it is our opinion that political agitation on the subject of a tariff upon iron should cease; that in all our efforts to secure the change which we ask for, we act only as business men, and that we stand ready to accept any fair compromise between the extremes of party, which will insure stability to the Iron interest, and fair remuneration to the labour and capital engaged in it.

On motion of Samuel J. Reeves, it was

Resolved, That this meeting recommend to the favourable consideration of those interested in the manufacture of iron, Mr. Frederick Overman's work on Iron, just published by Mr. Baird, of this city, as a valuable contribution to this department of science, and a useful compendium and guide to the iron-master in the practical operations and theory of making iron.

On motion of A. S. Hewitt, it was

Resolved, That J. S. Skinner has done most essential service to the true interests of our national industry, in his able Magazine, entitled "The Plough, Loom and Anvil;" and that this Convention heartily commend his course, and recommend his work to the warm patronage of the Iron trade.

On motion of Stephen Colwell, it was

Resolved, That this Convention, sensible of the ability with which the American Railroad Journal is conducted, approves the course of the same in reference to the industrial interests of the country, and commend it to the patronage of the Iron trade.

On motion of Stephen Colwell, the Convention adjourned *sine die.*

A General Committee was appointed to make the necessary arrangements to carry out the object of the Convention, and to appoint an Executive Committee, to which were referred the Reports of the Standing Committees and the Resolutions with instructions to publish and distribute, together with such other matter as they might deem interesting or important to the trade at this time.

THOMAS CHAMBERS,
President.

Charles E. Smith,
Nathan Roland,
Secretaries.

General Committee.

Stephen Colwell,	Abraham S. Valentine,
Robert Kelton,	John A. Wright,
Geo. P. Whitaker,	Edward B. Grubb,
Lindley Fisher,	Col. Jos. Paxton,
Charles E. Smith,	Isaac Eckert,
Robert Coleman,	M. Brooke Buckley,
Samuel J. Reeves,	James Hooven,
Thomas Chambers,	Joseph Whitaker,
Joseph Cabot,	Charles Brooke, Sr.,
Erskine Hazard,	Abraham Gibbons.

The Memorial reported by the proper Committee, will be found on the first page.

REPORT

OF THE COMMITTEE ON STATISTICS AND THE STATE OF THE TRADE.

It has been repeatedly asserted that the Iron manufacture of England has been established under a system of free trade; and it has been thence argued that a similar system should be adopted in the United States. This assertion, it is believed, has not been met in this country by a detailed statement of facts, and your Committee are of opinion that they cannot better discharge the duty confided to them, than by reporting a brief account of the rise and progress of the manufacture of Iron in England, with a history of the efficient protection extended to that manufacture not only during its infancy, but long after it had reached such a stage of maturity as to be able to maintain itself against foreign competition.

It will be seen by the evidence subjoined by your Committee, that, during a period of nearly a century and a half, a system of duties, some of which were not only prohibitory in their effect, but highly penal in their restrictions, was maintained; that during this long period, a series of brilliant inventions for the improvement of the manufacture of iron were introduced, and were sustained by means of the support furnished by government to the capitalists interested in this department of industry; and that it is only a consequence of this continued protection and of the improvements encouraged by it, that the Iron of England holds its actual position as a staple article of consumption and export. It will also be seen that years elapsed after the manufacture was supposed to have reached the stage of self-support, before it was considered safe or wise to remove the duties from imported Iron; that so firmly secured was the manufacture, that the proportion of imports did not increase after the repeal of the duties; and that notwithstanding this evidence, the prohibition upon exports of tools and machinery belonging to Iron works was continued, and re-declared as late as the year 1834.

Before introducing the details upon which the conclusions just stated are based, your Committee beg leave to make a few general observations.

The most striking feature of comparison between the legislation of Great Britain and that of the United States, is the steadiness of the former in the development of their domestic resources, and the encouragement of confidence on the part of capitalists, and men of enterprise; and the vacillation of our own measures. Our business, instead of being steady and regular, as it would be, is converted into a species of adventure, looked upon by the capitalist as more hazardous than any shipping or commercial speculation, however wild; for in any particular enterprise in commerce, even if there should be a loss, there remains a balance in cash. But to make iron there must be invested in buildings and machinery a capital greater than many of our merchants employ in their whole business. That investment should be regarded as a pledge to the government, of the confidence of the manufacturer in the stability and permanence of the existing laws affecting his business, and a pledge to the labouring man, of steady and regular employment, equally advantageous to the owner and the workman.

But how are the facts? The investment is no sooner made, and several hundred families gathered around the works, looking to them entirely for their support, than the law is changed, or what is almost as bad in its effects on all parties concerned, a change is *talked of.* Buyers reduce their orders—makers are obliged to dismiss their workmen and prepare for the threatened storm. Their credit is injured from the fact of having so large a portion of capital invested in their works, which, when standing idle, can only be regarded as so much money sunk or lost, as they pay no interest and cannot be sold.

But in addition to these evils, there is one attendant on these frequent changes, which, in reference to the progress and perfection of the manufacture, is quite as great as all the others.

There is no branch of manufacture that relies more, for its economical and profitable prosecution, on the division of labour, and the consequent skill of the workmen, than that of iron. Every man and boy employed in the rolling mill has his peculiar duty, and must have more or less tuition and training before he is capable of performing it. The iron passes through all their hands before it is finished. The awkwardness or ignorance of one of them will frequently destroy the product of the labour of twenty others, and entail a total loss of all that labour on the manufacturer. Again, no kind of manufactured goods can command a sale, unless it is of a uniform quality; even if that quality be inferior, it must be uniform. This can only be attained by experience and care in the management, by skill and constant practice in the workmen; by their being accustomed to the materials which they are using, as well as to work with, and for each other. With these advantages of drill and practice, we can produce iron cheaper every year, even if we pay the same price for labour and materials. But these advantages we are not permitted to enjoy. Our works are stopped, our men scattered to every quarter of the country; and then follows a long period of inaction and consequent distress amongst the families connected with the works. Meantime the alleviation of these evils is embarrassed, and the relations of the employer and the employed are embittered by the declarations of interested persons, who affirm that the cessation of employment is the result of a combination for political effect. We are denounced as tyrants, our men are stigmatized as slaves, and their worst passions are appealed to. Ingenuity is exhausted in the effort to show that the manufacturers of iron (a class composed of men of all shades of political and religious opinion, the largest portion of whom have never seen each other) have obstinately combined together to sacrifice present profits to the hope of extorting greater ones from the government. And that they are using miseries needlessly occasioned by them, to strengthen their appeals for public aid. If it could be asked of us seriously to reply to such assertions, it would be enough to point to the manufacturers who have become bankrupt within the last two years. Upon a resumption of business there is a scarcity of skilful men, and a consequent advance in their wages to onerous and unjust rates, beyond the ability of the manufacturer to pay. A whole year, at least, is consumed in arriving at the same degree of economy and perfection in the manufacture, as had been attained before the suspension of operations.

The constant and regular running of their works is a principal cause of the perfection and cheapness attained by the English manufacturers; and one, the results of which we might enjoy to a greater extent than they; for our workmen are more intelligent than theirs, and therefore susceptible of greater improvement. It is also the *principal reason* why they prefer to run at a loss, rather than stop. They have the requisite capital; we have not, and must stop or be ruined; and we naturally choose the lesser evil. It is against *this evil* that we ask the protection of our government.

Our progress from 1842, not only in the manufacture of iron, but also of hardware and other articles made of iron (in which the skill and ingenuity of our workmen can be brought in competition with those of English workmen, without the enormous difference in capital being so much felt), until we were arrested by the present ad valorem tariff, was without a parallel in any branch of manufactures in this country; our production of iron had reached a quantity equal to that of England 15 years ago (800,000 tons in 1834), and with the advantage of steadiness in the tariff, if one half the amount of protection extended to the English manufacturer were extended to us, your committee are clearly of opinion that in less than 10 years, n addition to supplying the entire home market, we should have iron to export.

1661. A petition was presented to the House of Commons, praying that a duty might be laid on foreign iron, but the House refused to grant it.

1679. The first duty was laid upon iron of 10s. per ton.

1710. The duty on iron imported in English vessels

		was	£2	1	6	per ton.
"	"	in foreign "	2	10	10	"
"	"	made in Ireland,	1	0	0	"

1740. There were 59 furnaces, producing 17,350 tons of iron per annum, or 294 tons each furnace; equal to 5½ tons a week to each furnace. Up to this time all the iron was made with charcoal.

1750. An Act of Parliament was passed to encourage the importation of pig-iron from the colonies, by taking off the duty of 3s. 9d. which had been heretofore levied on colonial pigs, the same as foreign iron. This was agreed to by the iron-masters, owing to the scarcity of charcoal, and it was argued, that as the country could afford no more charcoal for additional furnaces, they must either gradually abandon the manufacture, or take off the duty, and keep their charcoal for refining and manufacturing those pigs into bars, chains, and all finer articles, and for that reason the act also provided that no mill or other engine for slitting or rolling iron, or any plating forge to work with a tilt hammer, or any furnace for making steel, should be erected in the colonies, and those already erected should not be carried on.

The imports of American iron into Great Britain had averaged for the previous 10 years, 2,360 tons per year, and regularly increased until 1771, when they reached 7,525 tons, being rather more than 1–6th the total import of all kinds of iron into England at that time.

We add the copy of a letter from the officers of His Majesty's Dock-yard at Woolwich, to the Navy Board, dated September 3d, 1735: "We have lately received from his Majesty's yard at Deptford, barr iron flatts, of two and a quarter inches broad and half an inch thick, 15cwt. 0qr. 4lbs.; squares of seven-eighths of an inch, 5cwt. 0qr. 12lbs., imported by Mrs. Cowley, from America; and, pursuant to your warrant of the 11th July, 1735, have made sufficient tryal of each of the sorts, find the said iron to be very good, and fit for his Majesty's service, superior in every respect to the best Swedes iron, and in our opinion worth £17 10 6 per tun."

1760. Cast-iron blowing Cylinders were first used.

1769. Watt's first patent taken out for improvements in the steam-engine.

1775. Partnership of Boulton & Watt formed, and steam-engines applied to pumping mines and to the manufacture of iron.

1782. Duty on Iron raised to £2 16 2, being an increase of 14s 8d.

1783. Mr. Cort invented the process of Puddling, and consequently the substitution of mineral coal for charcoal in the manufacture of bar-iron.

1784. He invented the Rolling Mill.

The price of iron for a long period previous to this time had been pretty steady at from £17 to £18.

From this time should be dated the commencement of the present English Iron manufacture, as the preceding 24 years embrace all the inventions now in common use; inventions which entirely revolutionized the old system of making iron, and to which England owes the extent and cheapness of her manufacture at the present day. And from this time, also, is to be dated the commencement of her system of protection to her own manufactures and prohibition to all others, by which the domestic competition in 41 years enabled her to manufacture iron at prices defying all rivalry, when she throws open her ports and proclaims free trade or free competition, when the fact of her exporting iron to every kingdom in the world demonstrated that nobody could compete with her.

1785. It was prohibited to export any tools, engines, models or plans of machines used in the manufacture of iron, under a penalty of 1 year's imprisonment, £200 fine and the confiscation of the articles shipped or *intended* to be shipped. The same fine of £200 to be inflicted on the master of the vessel and on the custom-house officers, who were to be dismissed, and for ever to be incapable of holding any office under his Majesty. For enticing a workman, the penalty was 1 year's imprisonment and £500 fine for every workman so enticed; fine to be doubled on the second offence.

1787. The preceding act amended so as to allow tools used in the Iron manufacture to be exported to the West India Colonies, *except* Rollers, plain or grooved, and all other tools and utensils relating to the Rolling or Slitting mills, the punching of iron or casting or boring of cannon. The importation of Iron slit or hammered into rods, and Iron drawn or hammered less than ¾ inch square, and all wrought iron, except bars unwrought, hoops, and scraps, and all manufactures of iron and steel *prohibited.*

1788. There were 77 furnaces in all, producing 61,900 tons of Iron a year, being 804 tons to the furnace; being an increase in the yield of 173 per cent., owing to improved machinery and greater skill.

1795. The act of '86 prohibiting the export of tools and machinery, &c., was made perpetual.

1796. Duty raised to £3 1 9 per ton, being an advance of 5s 7d.—At this time there were 121 furnaces, producing 124,879 tons per annum, being 1,032 tons to the furnace; showing an increased yield of 28 per cent. in 8 years.

1797. The duty was raised to £3 4 7, being an increase of 2s 10d.

1798. " again raised to 3 15 5, " " 10s 10d.

1800. Tooke, in his work on "high and low prices," part IV, page 37, speaking of this period of the iron trade, says: "Thenceforward the produce of Iron in this country (Great Britain) proceeded so rapidly, that, with the aid of further duties, amounting almost to a prohibition of importation, it not only kept pace with the increasing demand, but has eventually nearly superseded the use of foreign iron in this country, and has furnished a surplus for exportation. The price of foreign iron, accordingly fell almost progressively, from 1801 till the close of the war (1815).

1801. The black band ore discovered in Scotland by Mushet. The same year he introduced a new system of coking the coal by which a saving of fuel was obtained.

1802. There were 168 furnaces, estimated to produce 170,000 tons.

1803.	Duty raised to £4 4 4½,	being an increase of		8s 11½d.
1804.	" 4 17 1	"	"	12s 8½d.
1805.	" 5 1 0	"	"	3s 11 d.
1806.	" 5 7 5¾	"	"	6s 5¾d.

At this time there were 227 furnaces in all, of which 167 were in blast, producing 258,206 tons per annum, or 1,540 tons to the furnace; showing an increased yield of 49 per cent. in 10 years.

1809. Duty raised to £5 9 10, being an increase of 2s. 4¼d.

1813. " 6 9 10, " " £1.

1814. Mr. Hill patents the use of puddler's and heater's cinder in the blast furnace instead of ore.

1818. Product this year estimated at 300,000 tons, showing an increase of 41,794 tons a year.

1819. Duty, if imported in English vessels, raised to £6 10 0 per ton.
" " foreign " " 7 18 6 "
Iron slit or hammered into iron rods, Iron drawn, or hammered less than ¾ of an inch square, (heretofore prohibited,) now admitted at a duty of 20 0 0 "
Pig-iron, heretofore charged a duty of 27½ per cent., now charged a duty of 17 6 "
Kinds not enumerated, heretofore prohibited, now admitted at a duty of 50 per cent.
Hoops heretofore charged £11 8 4 per ton, now charged £23 15 0 "

1820. Mushet computes the product this year at 400,000 tons being an increase of 141,794 tons on the make of 1806, or 55 per cent. in 14 years.

1823. Amount of Iron produced 452,066 tons, being an increase of 193,860 tons, or 75 per cent. in 17 years.

1824. Black band ore first used alone in the furnace, at Monkland, Scotland.

1825. There were 261 furnaces in blast.
103 " out "
———
363 " producing 581,367 tons,
being an increase of 129,301 tons, or 29 per cent. in 2 years; average yield per furnace, 2,228 tons; an increase yield per furnace of 45 per cent. in 19 years.

M. de Villefosse states the price of bar-iron at the works, in various countries, this year, to be

France, - - - - - -	Per ton £26	10
Belgium and Germany, - - -	" 16	14
Sweden, at Stockholm, - - -	" 13	13
Russia, at St. Petersburg, - -	" 13	13
England, at Cardiff, - - -	" 10	00

1826. Duty reduced to £1 10 on bars unwrought, being a decrease of £5.

Slit or hammered into rods reduced from £20 to £5.

Hoops, duty not changed, per ton £23 10 0.

Pig-iron, " 10 0.

Kinds not enumerated, 20 per cent.

We have now traced the English duties through 15 different changes, during a space of 147 years of unwavering protection, always under specific duties, and always increasing in amount, until they were no longer needed. We subjoin a list of the countries they shipped Iron to at this time, arranged in the order of the quantities they took respectively. It comprises every nation in the world—the United States standing second in quantity. In 1830 we became the largest customers and have remained so ever since.

	Tons.		Tons.
Asia,	12,631	Mexico and S. A. Republics,	2,317
United States,	12,491	Turkey and Egypt,	2,273
Italy,	9,435	Gibraltar,	1,601
France,	7,910	Spain,	1,493
British West Indies,	6,908	Africa,	1,411
N. A. Colonies,	6,067	Malta,	660
Portugal,	6,067	Denmark,	319
Netherlands,	4,759	Russia,	158
Brazil,	2,789	Norway,	94
Germany,	2,615	Prussia,	68
Foreign West Indies,	2,515	Sweden,	10

The imports of foreign Iron for consumption for the 10 years previous to 1826 averaged 9,729 tons, or 10½ per cent. of the exports of British Iron.

And for the succeeding 10 years of low duties, were 14,586 tons, being 10¼ per cent. of the exports of British Iron for the same period; showing that the duty had become a dead letter before it was taken off, as the imports of foreign iron, after the duties were taken off, did not quite maintain their proportion to the exports of British Iron. We subjoin a table of the imports and exports for 20 years before, and 20 years after the reduction of the duties, averaged for each period of ten years.

	Average Annual Amount.		Average Prices in England.		
	English Iron Exported.	Foreign Iron Imported and Consumed.	English Bars.	Swedes Bars.	Russian Bars.
	Tons.	Tons.	£ s. d.	£ s. d.	£ s. d.
Average for 10 years ending January 5th, 1806	29,447	35,541	18 10 8	21 9 6	19 8 0
1816	50,908	14,273	14 3 9	17 9 0	16 8 0
Duty Reduced, 1826	92,721	9,729	10 5 6	16 12 6	17 15 0
1836	142,996	14,586	7 8 9	14 10 0	18 10 0
1846	332,810	19,479	8 0 11	12 10 8	18 2 6

But every maker of Iron knows that English Iron and Swedes or Russian (forming 9-10 of their imports) cannot be regarded as competing articles. The latter Iron being all charcoal hammered bars is entirely used for purposes for which the English Iron is not fit, and is in fact a raw material to the English manufacturer of steel and other fine articles, and therefore it was against their interest ever to have had a duty placed on it. Mushet, "Iron and Steel," page 536, speaking of this difference says: "A variety of processes have been followed out to form a good quality of bar iron with coke pigs and pit coal; in no case has a uniform quality of bar iron been produced, able to cope for all uses with the superior marks of Russia and Sweden. We acknowledge with pain and humiliation our dependence upon other countries for our Steel Iron, and it is with regret we see every industrious exertion made to obviate this dependence, foiled by the nature of our fuel, or the defective qualities of our ores."

1829. Mr. Neilson, of Glasgow, patents the use of hot-blast, effecting a great saving in fuel.

1830. Total number of furnaces, 360, yield 678,417 tons.

1833. Hot-blast better understood, and raw coal substituted for coke in Scotland, effecting a further saving in fuel.

1834. The prohibition to export Iron rollers and tools, or machines belonging to Iron works and various other works, recited and confirmed; penalty, forfeiture of the goods.

1836. Iron made this year estimated at 1,000,000 tons.

1837. Mr. Crane smelts iron successfully with Anthracite coal and hot-blast.

1839. Mr. Mushet states the number of furnaces to be 377 mineral coal, and 1 charcoal, making 378; in all producing 1,248,781 tons.

1840. Number of works this year 490; out of blast 88; in blast 402; producing 1,396,400 tons.

This being the result of a careful personal inquiry by a gentleman extensively known in the trade, is believed to be very nearly correct.

This would give the annual product of each furnace 3,473 tons.

Hot-blast furnaces, 162

Cold-blast furnaces, 240

Coal consumed to the ton of iron in Scotland, 3 tons.
" " " " England and Wales 3 12 cwt.

1842. The association of Iron Masters of York and Derbyshire, estimate the decreased make of iron this year, at 22·1 per cent. on make of 1840, which would give, for the product this year, 1,087,700 tons.

1843. Mr. Buckley (member of Parliament for New-Castle) estimates the make this year at 1,215,350 tons, being a decrease on 1840 of 181,050 tons, or 13 per cent.

The greatest decrease is in South Staffordshire, where it amounted to 106,900 tons, or 24½ per cent. on their make in 1840.

Duty reduced on bars to		£1 0 0
"	hoops and rods,	1 10 0
"	pig iron,	5 0

1844. Amount of Iron made this year estimated at 1,210,000 tons.

1845. Make this year estimated at 1,512,500 tons.

1846. Duty on Iron taken off entirely.

1848. The Commissioner appointed by Parliament reports the make of Iron this year to be 1,998,568 tons as follows:

	Furnaces.			Product.	
	In Blast.	Out Blast.	Total No.	Average per week.	Total for the year.
				Tons. Cwt.	Tons.
North Staffordshire,	16	3	19	78 15	65,520
South do.	77	62	139	80 00	320,320
Yorkshire,	23	5	28	55 13	66,560
Derbyshire,	20	10	30	91 10	95,160
Shropshire,	28	6	34	60 14	88,400
Northumberland,	24	12	36	80	99,840
Scotland,	89	41	130	115	539,962
North Wales,	5	6	11	62	16,120
South do.	151	45	196	90	706,680
Total No. in Blast,	433				
" " out Blast,		190			
" " in the Kingdom,			623		
" " tons produced,					1,998,568

1849. The make this year may be set down at fully 2,000,000 tons. The cholera and the disturbed state of the continent have tended to depress prices, both to the manufacturer and the workmen; and the closing of so many of the continental markets for iron has forced the enormous quantity of 318,875 tons on our market, at prices below our cost of production.

Price of Rolled Bar Iron

each year since 1822.

in Liverpool.

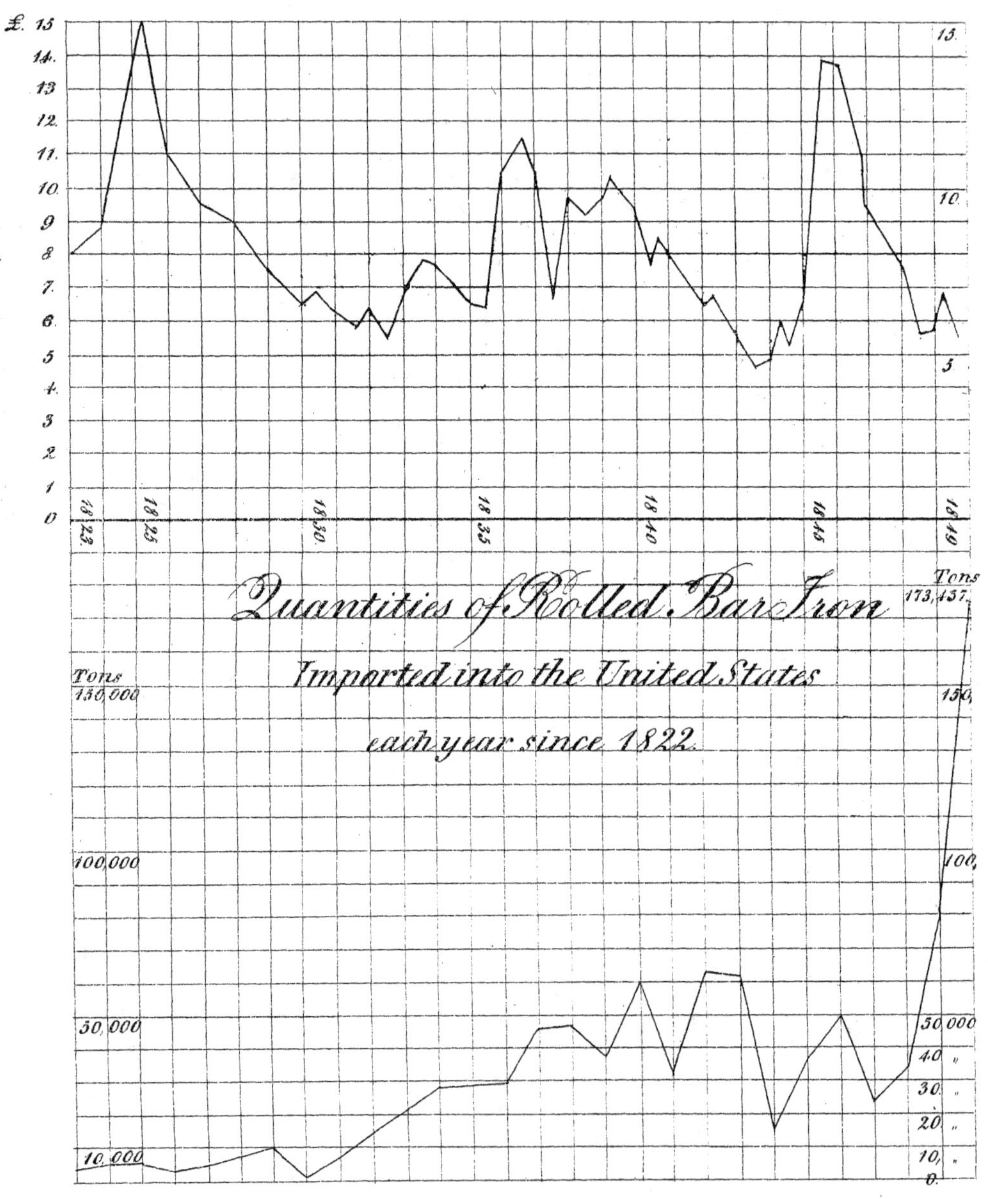

A. Kollner's Lith. Camp print. cor. of 2d and Dock St.

Price of Pig Iron

each year since 1822.

in Glasgow.

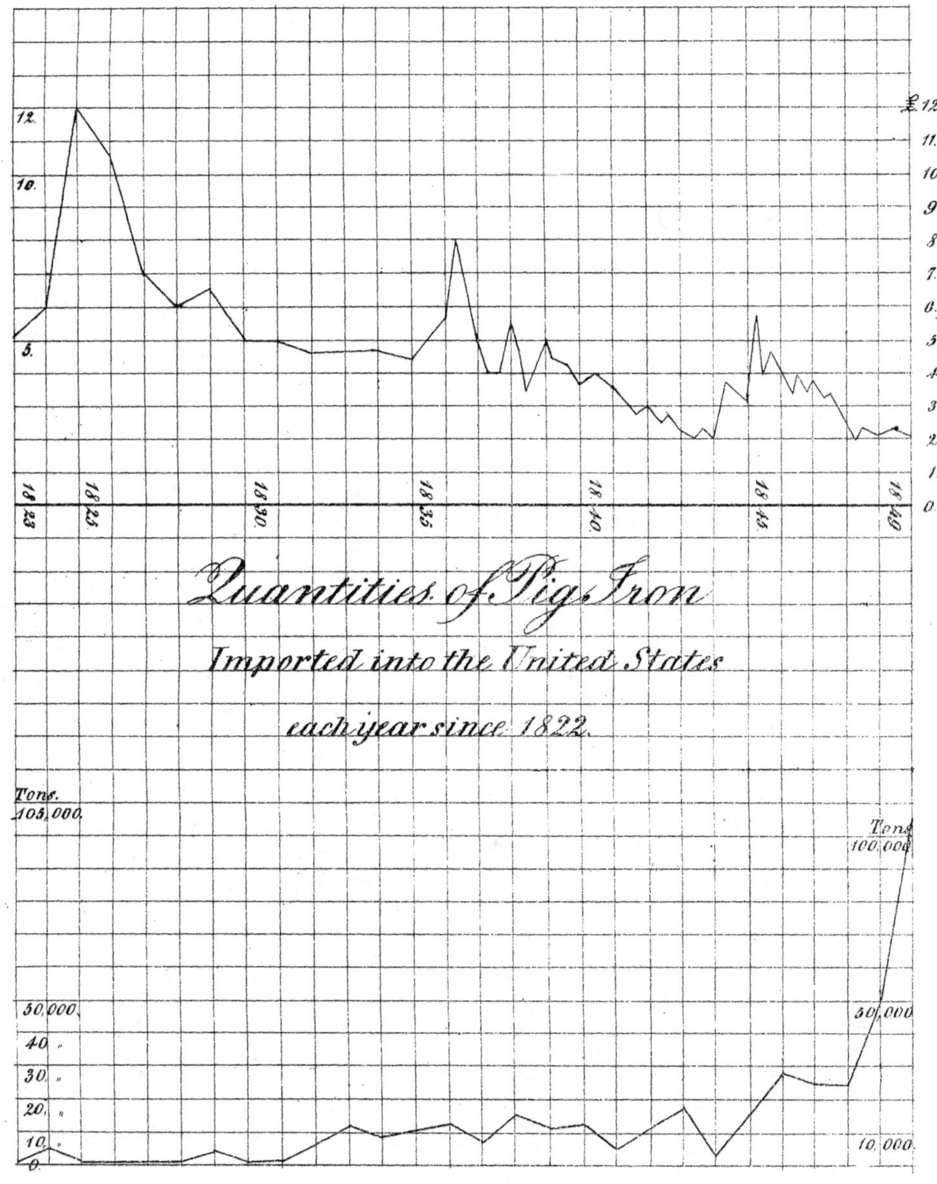

A. Kollner's Lith.y Camp. print. cor. of 2.d and Dock St.

We also present a statement of the quantities of pig and rolled bar iron imported into the United States each year from 1818, and the prices of the same at the shipping port, and two diagrams exhibiting the same information in a more striking form.

EXPLANATION OF THE DIAGRAMS.

Each space from left to right of the page represents one year. The dates are marked on the heavy straight line which runs across the middle of the page. Each space *above* this line represents £1 of the price; each space *below* it represents 10,000 tons of the quantity imported.

We conclude our report with a series of statements showing the cost to make pig-iron in Great Britain, and the cost of converting the same into rails, distinguishing the amounts paid for labour, fuel, &c.

STATEMENT OF THE QUANTITY OF PIG IRON IMPORTED INTO THE UNITED STATES, IN EACH YEAR SINCE 1818. TAKEN FROM THE REPORTS OF THE SECRETARY OF THE TREASURY.

Year.	Tons.	Cwt.	Value.
1818	198	10	
1819	331	14	
1820	329	4	
1821	917	16	
1822	1,180	14	
1823	2,480	7	
1824	792	16	
1825	815	9	$36,513
1826	1,704	12	67,004
1827	1,755	18	46,881
1828	3,496	17	93,025
1829	1,138	11	28,811
1830	1,124	19	25,644
1831	6,948	7	160,681
1832	10,151	5	222,303
1833	9,330	1	217,668
1834	11,113	5	270,325
1835	12,295	17	289,779
1836	8,541	2	272,978
1837	14,128	11	422,929
1838	12,191	10	319,099
1839	12,507	14	285,300
1840	5,515	14	114,562
1841	12,267	13	223,288
1842	18,694	1	295,284
1843	3,873	1	48,251
1844	14,944	0	200,522
1845	27,510	9	506,291
1846	24,187	16	489,573
1847	23,377	9	472,088
1848	51,632	1	815,415
1849	105,632	9	1,405,613

STATEMENT OF THE QUANTITY OF ROLLED BAR IRON IMPORTED INTO THE UNITED STATES EACH YEAR FROM 1818. TAKEN FROM THE REPORTS OF THE SECRETARY OF THE TREASURY.

Year.	Tons.	Cwt.	Value.
1818	2,698	19	
1819	2,564	10	
1820	2,969	5	
1821	2,184	4	
1822	5,066	14	
1823	5,346	13	
1824	5,790	9	
1825	4,250	10	$224,497
1826	4,437	1	223,259
1827	8,102	12	347,792
1828	10,294	17	441,000
1829	3,320	8	119,326
1830	6,949	1	226,336
1831	15,245	18	544,664
1832	21,837	5	701,549
1833	28,028	6	1,002,750
1834	28,896	7	1,187,236
1835	28,410	4	1,050,152
1836	46,675	14	2,131,828
1837	47,839	12	2,573,367
1838	36,174	6	1,825,121
1839	60,284	17	3,181,180
1840	32,828	14	1,707,649
1841	63,055	18	2,172,278
1842	61,599	5	2,053,453
1843	15,757	17	511,282
1844	37,891	4	1,065,582
1845	51,188	12	1,691,748
1846	24,108	16	1,127,418
1847	32,085	8	1,695,173
1848	81,589	6	3,679,598
1849	173,457	2	6,060,068

The Prices of Scotch Pig in Glasgow, from 1821 to 1849, inclusive.

Year.	Month.	Price. £	s.	d.
1821	January 1	7		
1822	" 1	6		
1823	" 1	5	5	0
1824	" 1	6	0	0
1825	" 1	12	0	0
1826	" 1	10	10	0
1827	" 1	7	0	0
1828	" 1	6	0	0
1829	" 1	6	10	0
1830	" 1	5	0	0
1831	" 1	5	0	0
1832	" 1	4	15	0
1833	" 1	4	15	0
1834	" 1	4	15	0
1835	" 1	4	10	0
1836	" 1	5	15	0
	" 8	6	0	0
	February 6	7	0	0
	March 19	8	0	0
	September 10	7	15	0
	November 1	7	0	0
1837	January 1	5	0	0
	June 8	4	0	0
	August 23	4	0	0
	October 16	5	10	0
1838	January 1	5	10	0
	April 1	5	0	0
	July 4	3	10	0
1839	January 10	5	0	0
	" 19	4	10	0
	September 20	4	5	0
1840	January 1	3	15	0
	September 10	4	0	0
1841	February 4	3	12	6
	September 10	2	17	6
1842	January 1	3	0	0
	August 1	2	7	6
	September 1	2	12	6
1843	January 1	2	5	0
	August 3	2	0	0
	October 3	2	5	0
1844	January 1	2	0	0
	April 26	3	10	0
1845	January 1	3	2	6
	March 14	5	12	6
	June 16	3	15	0
	October 3	4	15	0
1846	January 1	4	0	0
	April 1	3	6	0
	August 1	3	15	0
	November 1	3	9	0
1847	January 1	3	13	4
	May 1	3	5	3
	September 1	3	6	0
1848	January 1	2	8	4
	April 1	2	1	9
	July 1	2	5	6
1849	January 1	2	2	4
	April 27	2	5	0
	June 8	2	2	6
	September 28	2	5	0
	November 24	2	2	6

An account of the Selling Price of English Merchant Bar Iron in Liverpool from the year 1806 to 1849, both inclusive.

Year.	Month.	Price per ton.	Year.	Month.	Price per ton.	Year.	Month.	Price per ton.
1806	May	17 10 0	1816	August	9 10 0	1827	July	9 10 0
	July	17 0 0		October	9 0 0		December	9 5 0
	November	16 0 0		Do.	8 15 0	1828	January	9 0 0
1807	January	16 0 0	1817	February	8 10 0		March	8 15 0
	February	17 0 0		March	9 10 0		April	8 10 0
	March	16 10 0		June	9 10 0		Do. 25th	8 5 0
	July	16 0 0		July	10 10 0		May	8 0 0
	August	15 10 0		August	12 0 0		October	8 5 0
	September	15 0 0		October	13 0 0		December	7 15 0
1808	September	14 10 0	1818	February	12 15 0	1829	April	7 10 0
1809	January	15 10 0		April	11 15 0		June	7 5 0
	February	16 0 0		May	11 5 0		August	7 0 0
	March	15 0 0		June	10 15 0		October	6 15 0
	September	14 10 0		August	10 0 0		December	6 12 6
	October	14 5 0		September	11 10 0	1830	March	6 10 0
1810	January	14 10 0		December	12 10 0		June	6 15 0
	June	14 5 0	1819	May	11 10 0		October	6 10 0
	September	14 0 0		June and July	11 0 0		November	6 5 0
	October	15 0 0	1820	March	10 10 0	1831	May	6 2 6
1811	August	14 10 0		June	9 10 0		June	6 0 0
	September	14 0 0	1821	January	9 0 0		October	5 17 6
1812	May	13 13 0		February	8 15 0		December	6 5 0
	June	13 5 0		March	9 10 0	1832	May	5 15 0
	July	13 10 0		June	8 15 0		August	5 10 0
	October 1st	13 5 0		August	8 10 0		November	5 15 0
	Do. 22d	12 15 0	1822	January	8 0 0		December	6 5 0
	December	13 0 0		June	8 10 0	1833	February	6 15 0
1813	February	12 10 0	1823	July	8 0 0		April	7 0 0
	April	12 5 0		November	8 10 0		September	7 5 0
	June	12 0 0	1824	January	8 15 0		October	7 15 0
	December	13 0 0		July	9 15 0	1834	April	7 12 6
1814	February	13 10 0		September	10 0 0		May	7 0 0
	March	13 0 0		October 4th	11 0 0		August	6 12 6
	April	13 10 0		Do. 18th	11 10 0		September	6 10 0
	May	14 0 0		Do. 23d	13 0 0	1835	February	6 7 6
	June	13 15 0		November 24th	12 10 0		March	6 10 0
	August	13 10 0		December	13 0 0		June	6 7 6
	November	13 5 0	1825	January	14 0 0		August 1st	6 5 0
1815	February	13 10 0		February	15 0 0		Do. 31st	6 10 0
	May	13 0 0		March	14 10 0		September 16	7 0 0
	June	12 10 0		April	14 0 0		October 1st	7 10 0
	June 30th	12 0 0		August	13 0 0		Nov'ber 30th	8 0 0
	July 20th	11 10 0		Do.	12 10 0		December 8th	8 5 0
	August	11 0 0		September	11 10 0	1836	January	10 10 0
	December	11 10 0	1826	January	11 0 0		April 26th	11 10 0
1816	March	11 0 0		April	10 10 0		July	11 5 0
	April	11 15 0		May	9 10 0		October	11 0 0
	June	10 10 0		October	10 0 0		November	10 15 0
	July	10 0 0	1827	March	9 10 0		December	10 10 0
	Do.	9 15 0		April	8 15 0			

PRICE OF ENGLISH MERCHANT BARS IN LIVERPOOL, CONTINUED.

Year.	Month.	£. s. d.	Year.	Month.	£. s. d.	Year.	Month.	£. s. d.
1837	January 14	10 10 0	1841	April 3	7 15 0	1845	September 3	8 5 0
	February 24	10 5 0		" 19	7 12 6		September 26	8 15 0
	March 23	9 15 0		May 18	7 5 0		October 3	9 5 0
	April 15	9 15 0		June 3	7 0 0		December 3	9 0 0
	May 6	9 0 0		July 1	6 15 0	1846	January 3	9 0 0
	June 8	8 10 0		September 3	6 10 0		February 3	9 5 0
	July 15	7 5 0		November 18	6 7 6		March 17	9 0 0
	August 1	6 15 0	1842	January 1	6 10 0		June 18	8 10 0
	August 15	7 15 0		April 1	6 5 0		July 18	8 15 0
	August 23	8 10 0		May 3	5 15 0		August 17	9 0 0
	September 15	9 10 0		" 19	5 12 6		December 1	9 5 0
	October 16	9 10 0		June 18	5 10 0	1847	January 2	9 10 0
	November 23	9 5 0		August 1	5 7 6		February 2	9 10 0
	December 23	9 15 0		September 1	5 1 0		March 2	9 5 0
1838	February 7	9 10 0		" 8	6 0		June 3	9 0 0
	March 31	9 10 0		October 20	5 12 6		August 18	9 2 6
	June 4	9 5 0		November 3	5 10 0		September 18	9 0 0
	September 6	9 10 0		December 3	5 5 0		December 3	8 15 0
	December 14	9 15 0	1843	March 1	5 2 6		December 31	7 15 0
1839	January 10	9 15 0		April 3	5 0 0	1848	January 18	7 10 0
	" 19	10 5 0		June 16	4 10 0		February 11	7 12 6
	February 6	10 5 0		September 4	4 15 0		April 7	7 5 0
	May 17	10 0 0		October 3	5 0 0		May 12	6 15 0
	June 12	9 15 0		December 4	4 15 0		June 16	6 5 0
	September 20	9 10 0	1844	March 4	5 0 0		September 8	6 2 6
	November 15	9 7 6		April 4	5 5 0		October 13	6 0 0
1840	January 11	9 0 0		" 18	5 10 0		November 18	5 10 0
	February 18	8 15 0		May 1	6 0 0	1849	January 12	5 15 0
	March 31	8 10 0		August 3	5 5 0		February 9	6 2 6
	May 15	8 5 0		September 3	5 10 0		" 23	6 10 0
	June 30	8 0 0		December 3	5 15		March 23	6 12 6
	July 23	7 10 0		December 20	6 0 0		April 23	6 2 6
	August 29	7 15 0	1845	January 6	6 10 0		May 5	6 5 0
	September 3	8 5 0		February 3	7 10 0		" 25	5 10 0
	September 10	8 10 0		March 3	9 0 0		June 8	5 5 0
	November 14	8 5 0		April 3	10 0 0		August 3	5 10 0
	December 3	8 0 0		May 3	9 5 0		October 26	5 5 0
				June 3	8 5 0		November 24	5 10 0
				July 3	7 15 0			

STATEMENT

Showing the cost of making Coke Pig Iron in Wales.

	s. d.
1 ton of clay iron-stone,	10 0
1 " " cinder,	5 0
15 cwt. of red Hematite* ore from Whitehaven, at 22 shillings per ton,	16 6
3 tons of coal for coking, at 4 shillings,	12
17 cwt. " for the engine and hot blast, at 2 shillings,	1 9
10 cwt. limestone,† at 2 shillings,	1 6
Wages,	6 0
General expenses,	6 0
Cost at the furnace per ton,	£3 0 9

---

* As the price of this ore may be doubted by some persons, the items of cost are given as follows:

	s. d.
The price on board the vessel at Whitehaven, reduced in August '49 from 12s. to	11 0
Freight from Whitehaven to Cardiff,	7 0
Railroad from Cardiff to Merthyr, 25 miles,	2 6
Loading and unloading railroad wagons,	6
Tram way from railroad to furnaces, loading and unloading tram wagons,	1 0
Cost at the furnaces per ton,	£1 2 0

It is very generally used throughout Wales and Staffordshire, to mix with the clay iron-stone of the coal measures.

† At Merthyr the limestone costs about 1s. 6d. per ton, but along the valley above Newport it costs 4s. 6d. per ton. 3 shillings is given as the average.

In some places they use the blast furnace cinder for a flux instead of limestone, because of the high price of the latter. No account is taken of that, as the loss in the quality of the iron is more than the gain by using the cinder.

STATEMENT

Showing the cost of making Anthracite Pig Iron in Wales.

		£	s.	d.
2 tons of clay iron-stone,	at 10s.	1	0	0
15 cwt. Hematite ore	" 22s.		16	6
2 tons coal in the furnace	" 5s.		10	0
1½ " " steam, hot blast, roasting ore, &c."	5s.		7	6
10 cwt. limestone	" 3s.		1	6
Wages,			9	0
General expenses,			6	0
Cost at the furnace per ton,		£3	10	6

STATEMENT

Of the cost of making Pig Iron in Scotland.

		s.	d.
2 tons of raw coal,	4s.	8	0
3½ " " ore (equal to 1 ton 15 cwt. roasted,)	5s.	17	6
6 cwt. limestone,	7s.	2	1
Coal for engine and hot blast 1 ton,	2s.	2	0
Labour at the furnace,		5	0
General expenses,		5	8
Cost at the furnace per ton,		£2 0	3

STATEMENT

Showing the cost of converting Pig Iron to Rails, in Wales.

	PER TON. s.	d.	£	s.	d.
Assuming the cost f Pig Iron to be			3	0	9
Refining—Fuel, 10 cwt. coke at 9s.	4	6			
Wages, refiner and helper per ton,		11			
Breaking and wheeling metal to forge,		1¾			
13 per cent. loss on pig at £3 0 9	7	10¾			
Cost of fining,	13	5½		13	5½
" plate metal,	(*Carried over*)		£3	14	2½

Cost of Rails continued.

		(brought over)	£3 14 2½
		PER TON.	
Puddling—15 cwt. coal to puddler, at 4s.		3s. 0d.	
3 " " engine, at 2s.		8	
			3 8
Puddler and helper		6 0	
Squeezer		4	
Rolling puddled bar,		8	
1 extra boy at train, per day	2s. 2d.		
2 " " dragging out, at 11½d.	1 11		
2 men weighing,	3 6		
1 man wheeling cinder,	2 1		
	9 8÷30=	3 5-6	
Average quantity rolled per day, 30 tons.			
Ash fillers,		1-6	7 4
Loss 6 per cent. on plate, at	£3 14 2½		4 5½
Cost of puddling,	15 5½		
" puddled bar per ton,			£4 9 8

The top and bottom of the rail is made from puddled bar re-heated and rolled, which costs as follows:

Fuel—12 cwt. coal to furnace at	4s.	2 4¾	
3 " " engine at	2s.	8	
			3 0¾
Wages—Rolling per ton,		1 3½	
Heating "		1 8½	
			3 0
Loss 10 per cent. on puddled bar at £4 9 8			8 11¼
Cost of making tops and bottoms,		15 0¼	
Cost of tops and bottoms per ton,			£5 4 8¼

A rail pile is ¼ tops and bottoms at	£5 4 8¼		£1 6 2
¾ puddled bar	4 9 8		3 7 3
Cost per ton of rail piles,		*(Carried up)*	£4 13 5

Cost of Rails Continued.

				£	s.	d.
(amount brought up)				£4	13	5
Finishing Rails.						
Fuel—12 cwt. coal to furnace at 4s.			2s. 4¾			
3 " " engine at 2s.			8			
			——		3	0¾
Wages—Cutting, wheeling, and piling iron,			6d.			
Rollerman,			5			
Roughing down,			4			
Catching,			3			
Hooking in per day	2s. 9d.					
Heave up roughing, "	2 3					
" Finishing, "	1 6					
Catcher " "	2 0					
	8 6÷30=	3½				
Heating, including helper		1 8½				
1 extra helper to charge	2s. 6d.					
1 " coach	2 6					
	5 0÷30=	2				
Wages to heat and roll,		——			3	8
				£5	0	1¾
Sawing and hot straightening.						
1 man "	2s. 9d.					
3 men " 3s.	9 0					
1 man " 6s.	6 0					
30 tons per day,	23 9÷30=	10d.				
Filing saws,		¾				
Cold straightening,		10				
Dressing,		4				
Patching,		1				
Inspecting,		1¼				
Total—Hot and cold straightening and finishing,					2	3
Loss 10 per cent. at £4 13 5,					9	4
Cost of rolling and finishing per ton, 18 3¾						
(amount carried over)				£5	11	8¾

Cost of Rails Continued.

	£	s.	d.
(*brought over*)	£5	11	8¾
General Expenses—such as, superintendence of mills, engineers, firemen, masons, blacksmiths, fire-bricks, oil, grease, fuel for smiths, iron and steel to mend tongs, heater's and puddler's tools, sand, cinder and ore to line and repair the furnaces, renewal of castings burned and broken,		6	0
Cost at the mill,	£5	17	8¾
Freight from Merthyr to Cardiff,		2	6
Cost of 1 ton rails at Cardiff,	£6	0	2¾

STATEMENT

Being a summary of the preceding Statement, showing the cost of Fuel, Wages, &c., to the ton of Rails.

	Rate	s.	d.			£	s.	d.
Pig at						3	0	9
Fuel—Finery, 10 cwt. coke,	at 9s.	4s.	6d.					
Puddling furnace 15 cwt. coal,	" 4	3	0					
" engine 3 " "	" 2		8					
Tops and bottoms 12 "	4s.	2	4¾					
Engine 3 "	2		8					
		3	0¾	÷4=	9¼			
Rail finishing, furnace,								
12 cwt. coal	" 4s.	2	4¾					
2 " " engine	at 2		8					
Total cost of fuel to the ton of rails,							12	0
Wages—Finery,		1	0¾					
Puddling and rolling puddled bar,		7	4					
¼ wages tops and bottoms, 3s.÷4=			9					
		9s.	1¾d.			£3	12	9

Cost of Fuel, Wages, &c., to Ton of Rails Continued.

(*amounts brought over*,)	9s.	1¾d.	£3	12	9
Heating and rolling rails,	3	8			
Straightening and finishing rails,	2	3			
Total cost of labour to the ton of rails,				15	0¾

This amount was reduced 10 per cent. on account of the selling price of Rails going below cost—15s. 0¾d. less 10 per cent., or 1s. 6d.= 13s. 6¾d., which is the present actual cost of labour per ton of rails finished.

Losses in Manufacture.					s.	d.			
Finery, 13 per cent. on Pig at	£3	0	9	=	7	10¾			
Puddling, 6 per cent. on Plate at	3	14	2½	=	4	5½			
¾ tops and bottoms 10 per cent., on puddled bar at	4	9	8	=	2	2¾			
Rails, 10 per cent. on rail piles,	4	13	5	=	9	4			
Total cost of losses,							1	3	11
General expenses as before,								6	
Cost of the mill,							£5	17	8¾
Freight,								2	6
Cost of 1 ton Rails at Cardiff,							£6	0	2¾

STATEMENT

Showing cost to import Iron under the Tariff of 1846. *The charges being the average for* 10 *years on those actually paid by a large importing house.*

Cost as per Statement, £6 0 0,	$26 67
Commission for negotiating payment,	27
Shipping Charges,	56
Exchange 9 per cent.,	2 47
Duty,	8 25
Insurance,	41
Freight,	3 50
Portage,	50
	$42 63

STATEMENT

Showing difference in cost in English and American labour in the

ROLLING MILL.

	American price of Labour, 1849, per ton.	English price of Labour, 1848, per ton,	English price of Labour less reduction of 10 per ct. 1849, per ton.
	$	s. d.	$
Puddler and his helper, - -	3 50	6 0	1 29½
Rolling the puddled bar, - -	72¾	8	14½
Sundry labour, - - - -	82¼	1 8¾	37½
Shearing Iron for piles, - -	21	6	11
Heater and his helper, - -	87½	1 8½	37
Rolling, - - - - - -	85	1 11½	42
Straightening and finishing, - -	1 37½	2 3	48½
Sundry labour, - - - -	1 25½	3	5½
American labour to ton Iron, -	$9 61½		
English labour to ton Iron, 1848,		15 0¾	
English labour to ton Iron, 1849, since the reduction in wages, and the amount converted to Federal money, - - - - - - -			$3 25½

This does not show the *entire labour* in the rolling mill to the ton of Iron, as in England they include engineers, overseers, firemen, masons, &c., &c., with materials, grease, oil, &c., all under the head of General Expenses.

To make the American account correspond, these items have been omitted:

They amount to - - - - - - - - -	$1 38½
Add as above, - - - - - - - - - -	9 61½
American cost of labour, - - - - - -	$11 00
And by proportion the English labour, - - -	$3 71

Or very nearly ⅓ the amount paid in this country.

Extract from a Letter from John A. Wright, Esq.

GENTLEMEN:

In accordance with your request, I will lay before you concisely a fair statement showing the present state of the manufacture of Iron from the ore, and of the results which might fairly be anticipated from an encouragement of the business and the advantages consequent to this region of country, at the same time noticing the effects of the late revulsions in the Iron trade in this and adjoining counties.

There are probably few counties in the State richer in valuable ores than Mifflin, Huntingdon, and Centre. The ores are generally the richest hydrates, making the Iron so long and favourably known throughout the country as the Juniata Iron—equalled by some rare banks, but unequalled in extent of ore in the United States. This ore is generally found in the heavy limestone valleys; expensive to raise, being generally found in nests, seldom in regular veins or strata.

For the manufacture of Charcoal Iron these counties are admirably situated. The great ranges of mountains running parallel to the Allegheny, furnish immense bodies of woodland, unfit for cultivation, only rendered valuable by the wood, the growth replacing itself every twenty years. On these mountains, of which we count twelve ranges in the counties named, the wood is admirably calculated for charring, making strong and economical coal.

Fluxes proper to be used are abundant. Limestone in all its varieties is found, and each locality can furnish a suitable stone to flux the various impurities found in the ores.

You thus observe, these counties have within themselves sources of great wealth hardly touched. Though furnaces and forges have been in operation here for the last seventy-five years, yet, comparatively speaking, the business has not been very much extended. The varying and frequent changes in the market have at all times rendered it an uncertain business, to a great extent deterring capital from embarking in it. There has been no employment in this State that has met with so many revulsions, ruined so many fortunes, impoverished so many families, and in which so few fortunes have been made, (in our country acceptation of the term,) as in the manufacture of Pig-iron, and this from two causes already indicated: 1st, the unstable policy of the government, and 2d, the want of capital.

In the county of Mifflin there are 5 furnaces and 2 forges. All are out of blast but Freedom Forge.

In the county of Union there are 3 furnaces; 2 are out of blast, and the last, I understand, will blow out, unless there is some speedy change in the Iron market.

In the county of Huntingdon there are, to my knowledge, 4 furnaces and 1 forge out of blast.

In the county of Centre there are 4 furnaces out of blast, two forges and 1 boiler plate mill standing idle, leaving but 5 furnaces in blast in the county, and these are generally connected with extensive rolling mills, thus enabling them to go on as long as their united works pay expenses.

Much the largest portion of Iron made in Huntingdon County goes west to Pittsburg, many of the establishments being connected with mills in that city. But the furnaces dependent on the East for a market are stopped, with the exception of one or two furnaces. You will particularly bear in mind, that this is the state of things at the places where the iron made is almost exclusively of the best character, superior to any iron imported from England or Scotland, and fully equal to the best from Russia, Sweden, or Norway.

Were the Iron of ordinary character, not one furnace, forge, or mill could run one hour, without heavy loss. Such is the present state of the three counties of Mifflin, Huntingdon, and Centre. But to the *future.* At the present, and with the prospective prices of Iron, no money can be made in the manufacture of Pig-iron for market, in the counties named. Should Iron recede any more in price, a reduction any revolution may at a moment produce, more works must stop; and it is not only stopping, but to any one at all acquainted with the machinery of making Charcoal Iron, a *heavy loss* invariably following a stoppage of works is an unavoidable result. The reason of it is not difficult to understand. The necessary preparation of stock for a blast, including ore, amounts to a large sum of money. In addition is the heavy amount of stock in horses, teams, and fixtures. These fixtures are almost valueless to any one but the iron master. His stock has to be in course of preparation 20 months before it is used; and he lays out of the money invested in this way, before it is turned into Pig-iron, at least an average of 10 months. A year's stock is worth from $25 to $35,000. It is evident how he would lose if he has prepared stock under one situation of affairs, and before that stock is brought even into a useful shape, an entire change has come over the market, and he may find himself obliged to work this stock up, with loss staring him in the face. After this comes sacrifice on his stock, the workmen become scattered, and where life once appeared, all is still as death. In case of a revival of business at a later period, all these things must be purchased afresh, and at full cost. Men must be collected, and before one ton of Iron is made a large amount of money must be expended. These losses are serious matters, and go to increase the cost price of the Iron made, and to prevent that reduction in cost of making which an established business would insure.

Let us survey for a moment the effect on any or all the counties named, in the points of manufacturing, mercantile, and agricultural wealth.

The average number of men employed at a charcoal furnace making 1,000 tons pig iron per year is not less than 70; making a population immediately dependent of not less than 350. The average number of horses and mules is not less than 50. The amount of grain used will not vary much from 2,500 bushels wheat, 3,000 bushels corn, 3,000 bushels oats, 1,000 bushels rye, 80 tons hay, 3,000 bundles straw. The amount of merchandise sold near $8,000. In addition there is a vast amount of bacon used, and the farmer finds a market for all the vegetables and truck he will raise—his butter, eggs, veal, potatoes, &c., articles which will not bear transportation to market, and what is no unimportant item, saving a large quantity of manure to be used at home to enrich the soil.

Another advantage to the agricultural interests of this state is in the erection of furnaces far in among the mountains, prior to this known only to the hunter and trapper. The necessary clearing of land for coal, opens many rich tracts of land, thus saving the farmer a heavy expense, at the same time making a market for his productions at home; and land worth but from $1 to $5 per acre, prior to the erection of the furnace, is, in two or three years, worth from $40 to $50. This is no fancy sketch; every farmer in the three counties can point to such places. But in continuation of the idea above, let us take the consumption stated and apply it to Mifflin County, to four furnaces and one forge, now out of blast. The amount consumed, of articles which generally bear transportation, would be

12,000	bushels	wheat,
14,000	"	corn,
14,000	"	oats,
4,750	"	rye,

not including straw, 380 tons hay and bacon, and including corn and oats, which do not always bear transportation, and which sometimes find a better market at home than at the sea-coast. By referring to Canal Commissioner's Report for 1849, page 48, you will notice the whole amount shipped from Lewistown, the port of collection for all Mifflin, part of Centre, and part of Huntingdon Counties, was but

28,731	bushels	corn,
12,577	"	oats,
156,564	"	wheat,
19,635	barrels	flour.

Had the furnaces and forge been in operation, not one bushel of corn or oats would have been shipped, and but 60,000 bushels wheat from Mifflin County. But in place of 4 furnaces, Mifflin County is susceptible of sustaining in wood and ore at least 40 furnaces. And what would be the effect of this? An increase in production of corn, which pays much better at 50 cents per bushel than wheat at 100 cents per bushel. The increase of population that would ensue, amounting to 18,000 persons, would probably be as great as the agriculture of the county could support, without exporting one bushel of its product. The same arguments may be applied to the other counties named. Now what will be the difference to the agricultural interests of the counties named? Stop all the furnaces, as stop they must, and all the coarse grains and truck are lost, and the farmer is forced to export his wheat and corn in direct competition with the West, causing an unstable market, thereby destroying the value of land, from the uncertainty of the value of its productions. But this is not all. In old counties (old comparatively with the West), there is always a large labouring population depending for support on the demand for labour in the county. Stop the iron works, and you throw this labour on the farmers for support. With the highest average prices of grain, the farmer cannot afford to pay over 50 cents per day, and such is now the rate. Throw more labour, and you reduce the wages to the lowest standard. What is the effect of this? Not that the farmers grow rich, but that land depreciates in value, and grain in price, as more will be grown, and at less cost; or, what is the same thing, these men must go West and become producers, and thereby competitors, and prices of grain and land recede. The inevitable effect then of the stoppage of furnaces is an injury to the farmer, and every sensible farmer in the three counties will tell you the same, for they have been taught by sad experience.

But still this is not the whole extent of the injury. The capital employed in the erection and prosecution of Iron Works is greater than is generally imagined. You may rely that the following estimate does not exceed the truth:

First cost of building a Charcoal Furnace, with all the necessary outbuildings, in the most economical manner, is not less than	$20,000
For a Furnace making 1,000 tons metal per year will require, to keep up for ever, at least 7,000 acres, counting risk by fire, &c., at $1 per acre,	7,000
Capital invested in teams and necessary outfit,	10,000
Capital required to conduct business,	20,000
Total capital required,	$57,000

Destroy the Iron trade, and the works are valueless. No property depreciates faster in value. For the county of Mifflin alone, here is a loss of at least $170,000 capital in a few years. Apply this to the three counties, and the amount is enormous; but apply it to the State, and it becomes almost incalculable. The injury done then is to every class of people. The adventurous capitalist is probably ruined; the mechanic, the labourer, the farmer, and the State are deeply injured.

In the present state of the trade there is nothing but gloom. How perfectly impossible it is for Iron works to be carried on in this region of our State, you may judge from these facts:

The average actual cost of 1 ton of Pig Iron at the Furnace Bank in the 3 counties, is	$20 00
There is an average cost to convey the Iron to canals of	1 00
Average freight to market, Philadelphia or Baltimore,	5 25
Expenses in either city, commission at 2½, weighing, &c., interest,	1 25
Making cost in city,	$27 50
Now take capital as above estimated equal to $57,000, and make of 1,000 tons at 10 per cent. profit, (which will, considering the risk of fire, &c., not warrant any one in carrying on such works,) would be $57 00 or $5 70 per ton,	5 70
Requiring a price equal to	$31 27 per ton,

now worth in Philadelphia but $25 per ton.

And you will find this is not far wrong. If Iron masters would calculate the injury of property, destruction of woodland, wear and tear, at a proper and business valuation, many now counting an annual profit would find it was an *annual loss.* There can be no Pennsylvanian who has taken the trouble to examine the present state of the manufacture of Iron, but will, without regard to former notions, conclude that their success is identified with the prosperity of the State; and as they suffer communities suffer, and the State also, as it represents the whole body of the people. In these views I am supported by the vast majority of this section. Your success in securing such action of Congress as will benefit this suffering interest will meet with a hearty welcome.

Yours, very truly,

JNO. A. WRIGHT.

Freedom, Jan. 28, 1850.

THE IRON TRADE.

In our columns to-day will be found a very valuable communication on the production of Iron in this country; and the rate of duties which is necessary to sustain that important interest on a reasonable basis. The names appended to it will be a sufficient guarantee both for the intelligence and candour with which it is written, and for the general correctness of the facts stated. We trust it will receive attention from the Committee of Congress having charge of the subject of revenue duties, for we can assure them that among all the arguments and statistics which will doubtless be pressed upon them by the Iron masters, none will be more worthy of respectful consideration. The views of the writers will be acceptable to the Democratic members of Congress, in this particular at least, that they propose no change in the *mode* of assessing duties, but only the adoption of a sliding scale in respect to this particular interest, while the duties themselves shall continue to be ad valorem, as at present. It is unnecessary to add, that by the above remarks we do not mean to endorse every position taken by the writer.—*Journal of Commerce.*

For the Journal of Commerce.

Sir:—Your articles on Iron have attracted universal attention, and especially of many who are largely interested in its manufacture, as indicating the policy which would meet the chief difficulties in the way of placing that important branch of our national industry on a substantial basis. The spirit of your articles was such as to render it incumbent upon the domestic iron trade to make their condition and wants fully known, or to cease their complaints. With the view of furnishing you with exact data, we should have addressed you some time since, had not the Pittsburg Iron Convention marked out a line of policy which was contrary to our experience and convictions;—and as we did not desire to assume an antagonistic position to the trade at large, we have delayed making the statement, which is due to the public, until the Iron interest on the Atlantic coast had expressed its views. This was done by the Philadelphia Convention, on the 20th inst.; and its resolutions, embodying the views of the great majority of the trade, take such ground as justify the statement we now place before you.

And first: *What is the real condition of the domestic Iron trade?* Is it actually depressed, and threatened with ruin, or does all the outcry proceed from men who, having realized "princely fortunes" annually, are now clamorous because their profits are reduced to reasonable limits; or from anotherclass, who, having erected works in improper locations, desire not so much to *make Iron* cheaply, as to build up villages, and speculate in real estate?

Undoubtedly, to some extent, there are such cases; and further, there are one or two positions in the country which combine such extraordinary natural advantages with every superior quality, as to make them almost independent of legislation; but as to the *great fact*, that the great majority of establishments, judiciously located, and managed with proper skill and economy, have been compelled to suspend work, throughout the land, for want of remunerating work, there cannot be a shadow of doubt.

To correct a prevailing error, let it be premised that this country *exports* little or no iron. The exportation of nails, to which your Journal lately referred, consisted of a few casks, shipped by an American provision house, as an experiment, for coopering pork barrels in Liverpool; and it is absurd to suppose that such a trade will ever be worth a second thought. So, the exports of iron, to which the Evening Post referred a few days since, really consists of *machinery*, sent to the Spanish colonies and South America, and are only kept up by the superiority of the American Sugar Mills. So again, a few tons of pig-iron have at various times been sent to England, (by the writers among others,) for the purpose of being tried for steel; the raw material for which Great Britain now imports from Sweden, at very high prices. The discovery of such an iron in this country, would undoubtedly lead to its exportation—but such a result has not yet been reached, and even if it had been, it would be due not to our capacity to produce iron *more cheaply*, but to the impossibility of making it in England at all, from the want of suitable ore. We have, therefore, only a home market, and when that is closed, the Iron trade is prostrated.

There are two great interests at work on iron—the one producing *pig* iron, and the other making *bars*. The manufacture of the former subdivides itself into two classes; the one using *charcoal* as the fuel, and the other employing *mineral* coal. Charcoal iron is more expensive to produce, but generally has the advantage in quality, and for many purposes commands a higher price. Its cost to the maker, on tide water, ranges from $25 to $30 per ton. Iron made with mineral coal, on the contrary, can be delivered on tide water (in all our calculations we refer to well located establishments) at a cost ranging from $17 to $20 per ton.

The *market* for both kinds of iron, has been to a considerable extent for remelting in the foundry, but *chiefly* for being converted into wrought iron. For this latter purpose they have not had, to any extent, to encounter foreign competition, because forge pig-iron cannot be delivered here from England duty free, any cheaper than it can be produced here. But as will be seen hereafter, the market for forge pig-iron, being almost entirely cut off, by the stoppage of the rolling mills, the foundries have had all the pig-iron crowded into them—and as a matter of course, the supply being far in advance of the demand, was alone a sufficient cause to produce prices ruinously low. But, for foundry purposes, in addition, the competition with *Scotch* pig-iron had to be met, which, duties off, can be delivered in New York at a cost not exceeding $14 to $16 per ton. This competition, of course, is ruinous to the charcoal furnaces, and, aided as they are by the duties on foreign iron, the anthracite furnaces have had a desperate struggle to keep in blast.

The difficulty, then, with the makers of pig iron, is not so much the mode of assessing duties on *pig*, as the *want of a market* for their forge iron, in the rolling mills; and if that market can be reopened, the complaints from this quarter will, we believe, cease.

For the production of bar iron of equal quality from pig iron, we start on an equality with Wales; in other words, the forge pig iron can be made here at a rate not materially greater than there—except charcoal iron, which generally makes a superior bar iron and commands a better price.

The finished bar iron, however, costs much more to make here than in Wales, and this is chiefly due *now*, to the higher price of *labour* in this country. The difference in the first cost of a ton of railroad iron, we cannot estimate at less than fifteen dollars. The expense of delivery in New York from well located works in this country, and from Wales, does not materially differ;—so that, with a duty much less than $15, when, to keep their works in operation, both foreign and domestic makers are willing to sell at cost, our mills are compelled to suspend work. Such is the present state of things—for the duty ranges from $7 to $10, according to the quality of the iron. The consequence is, that the rolling mills of the country are now idle, with the exception of the nail works, which have become almost independent of Tariff, because the superiority of the raw material used, enables them to produce nails with much less labour than is necessary abroad. A few merchant mills are also kept in motion, from the absolute necessity of having a certain amount of iron of superior quality for fine work; but of fifteen rail mills, only two are in operation, doing partial work, and that only because their inland position secured them against foreign competition, for the limited orders of neighbouring railroads—and when these are executed, not a single rail mill will be at work in the land.

Such then, without any disguise, and to the best of our knowledge, is the real condition of the Iron interest of the country. The manufacture of bar iron is prostrated by foreign competition, and the manufacture of pig iron is in the same condition, from the consequent loss of its usual and legitimate market.

In this state of things, when it is apparent that, without some action of the government, the business cannot be sustained, except to a very limited extent, the question naturally presents itself, whether the production of iron is of sufficient importance to the community, to call for any legislative interference at all in the premises.

In the first place, it is essential that the national government should be supplied with iron of the best quality, and of *domestic* manufacture, as it would never do in time of war to rely upon foreign countries for a supply of this indispensable engine of defence. This consideration is met by the fact that, as the government buys only American iron, and pays the highest price for the best article, furnaces adequate to supply its wants will, in any event, be kept in operation.

The next consideration arises out of the immense quantity of iron which is annually consumed in this country, amounting, at the present low prices, to at least forty millions of dollars, of which from one-fourth to one-third only has been imported during the last year, yet regulating the price of the whole quantity, for it is a law of trade that the *small* quantity makes the market price. Now if the production of iron ceases in this country, and an additional demand for twenty-five to thirty millions of dollars, making *three* times our present demand, be thrown upon the English market, the price must advance enormously—far beyond the rate at which, if the domestic manufacture had not ceased, American iron would have been supplied. The *consumer* will be the first to call for a *domestic production* of *sufficient* extent, at any rate, to keep the price of foreign iron in check. We do not wish to be understood as predicting an entire discontinuance of the manufacture of iron, because in the interior the expense of transportation affords a very handsome protection, as far as the local consumption is concerned; but we do say, that the day is rapidly approaching when, if no steps are taken to retain the skill which we have been many years in obtaining, and are fast losing, the *consumer* will have substantial reasons to regret that he did not retain the *protection* against the exactions of foreign makers, which a large domestic production on the seaboard has for many years afforded.

But there is another difficulty attending the importation of a largely increased amount of iron. How are we to pay for it? Already we send all the cotton, grain, provisions, and tobacco which the foreign market will bear, and the exportation of more will only serve to break down the price, so that additional exportation will produce no more money in the aggregate. There is a limit to which we can pay in government and state stocks, and railroad bonds—a mode of payment which, by the way, has been adopted to a fearful extent during the last year. The balance must finally go forward in specie—and if this mode of settlement last long, then come bank contractions, cessation of business, bankruptcy of weak houses, and the countless embarrassments which result from being in debt without the means of payment. Bankers, merchants, mechanics, and men of all ranks, would cry aloud for such a production of iron as would be required to stop the shipments of specie.

These would seem, then, to be good reasons why, for the sake of the *consumer*, and the *business community* at large, as well as the *producer*, the iron business should be sustained so as to keep up a *fair competition* with the foreign article, and insure such a domestic supply as shall serve to prevent prices from reaching extravagant points, and the country from being annually saddled with debts which can only be discharged at the expense of its permanent prosperity.

Having then shown that the iron business actually needs relief, and that the whole community is interested in affording it, if its wants are moderate, let us see what its precise difficulties are before we suggest the remedies.

English iron can be made cheaper than American, not because *less labour* is required, but because that labour *costs only one-third as much.*

To appreciate this difficulty fully, let us examine of what the cost of a ton of iron is made up in this country. A complete establishment for the manufacture of 15,000 tons of bar per annum, has been built in this country, during the last five years, at a cost for ore beds, furnaces, and rolling mill, of about $600,000. The interest of this sum at 7 per cent. (in England 3 per cent. would be sufficient), is $42,000, or less than *three* dollars per ton. The remaining cost consists in mining ore and coal, which is done by men,—the hauling and boating to the works, done by men and horses,—the manufacture into pig and the conversion into bar iron, all done by men, because the machinery has been allowed for in the interest account; the repairs made to the machinery, all done by men; so that the whole cost of a ton of bar iron, with the exception of $3 interest on fixed capital, and about $4 paid for tolls on canals and railroads, consists of money paid for the labour of men and horses. Now what is done with this money? With the exception of a small portion, which each labourer strives annually to add to his little saving fund to provide against accidents, and the bodily decay to which he, of all men, is most subject, it is all paid out for food and clothing, which comes directly or indirectly through the mechanic from the farmer.

Now, then, if we must make iron in this country in competition with English labour, it is very clear what must be done. *The labourer must take less wages,* in other words, he must not *think* of a savings fund; then, like the English operative, he must eat less meat, and use inferior food; and then his wife must dispense with all the little comforts that make home *home;* and then his children must be imprisoned in the cotton factory as soon as they can walk, instead of going to school; and he must finally become almost as soulless as the machinery he guides. But the labourer protests against any such degradation, and the farmer against any diminution in the consumption of his products; and humanity protests against the whole scheme, as a step backwards, and as shocking to the Christian spirit of the age.

There is still another resource. The farmer and the mechanic, who supply the wants of the iron maker, and get in exchange nearly all he earns, can charge less for what they furnish him, and thus enable him to work for less, and still keep his savings funds, and his home comforts, and his children at school. But against this remedy *the farmer and mechanic* protest, as depriving them of *their* hard earnings, already small enough.

Since, then, neither the labourer nor the farmer can be reduced to the proper point, the business can be given up altogether. But against this the consumer protests, because it will leave him at the tender mercies of the foreign makers—and the merchant protests against it, because the payment abroad for so much iron, would derange the whole business of the country.

There is but *one* remedy left; to impose such a duty on foreign iron as shall counterbalance the difference in the price of labour, first deducting from that difference any advantage which the American maker may have in the expense of getting his iron into market. Such a duty would not prohibit foreign iron. It would not give a monopoly of the market to the American manufacturer; but it would establish a *fair competition*, and in the struggle that would ensue, the *consumer* would be sure to reap the harvest, in the gradual improvement of the quality and cheapening of the cost, on the average of years, of this great staple article.

To provide this remedy, it is, fortunately, not necessary to build up a new commercial system, for all civilized governments, (whether wisely or not, on other grounds, it is not now necessary to discuss,) raise their chief revenue from duties on imports. These duties, where there is a direct competition between the foreign and domestic makers, undoubtedly *for the moment* operate as a tax upon the consumer; but the tax is necessary for the support of the government; and if it so happens that this unavoidable revenue tax is adequate to build up a domestic production sufficiently large to operate as a perpetual check upon the price of the foreign article, and insure the lowest possible average cost, then would the consumer and the government act most unwisely, if the tax were not so framed as to produce this desirable result. In other words, as the tax must be paid, the consumer is deeply interested in having it put in such a shape as will contribute, if possible, to the cheapening of what he consumes. The late Secretary of the Treasury, whose authority on this point will hardly be disputed, has reported that *forty* per cent. is the revenue standard for iron. The true cost of iron to the consumer is not the price of to-day, or of last year, but its average price for a series of years. Now, the average price of bar iron in Liverpool, from 1820 to 1849, and for each period of ten years during that time, has been just £8.

We do not hesitate to declare, that an ad valorem duty of 40 *per cent., the revenue standard, on* £8, *the average cost, will compensate for the difference in the price of labour, and be entirely adequate to build up such a domestic production of iron, as, without excluding the foreign article from our markets, to keep a check upon its price, and insure, on the average of years, the lowest possible price to the consumer.*

At this point, in fact, the interest of the iron maker and the iron consumer becomes *mutual.*

But here we are met by another difficulty. The price of English iron is not permanent at £8. It only *averages* that price. It sometimes rules as high as £15, as in 1846, and falls as low as £4 10s., as in 1849. And to this fact is due the great objection to the present mode of assessing duties; for, when the price falls below £8, the duty falling in equal ratio, becomes inadequate to compensate for the difference in the cost of labour. But, objectionable as it is to the iron maker, at the extreme point of depression, the system cannot prove less so to the government, as a *revenue measure,* when the regular fluctuations which have always taken place in the price of iron carry it up to the highest limit, as the duty will then become *prohibitory,* and the revenue will cease. So that not only iron makers, but revenue makers, are interested alike in modifying the present system.

Before, however, we appeal to the government, we are bound to show that there is no *natural remedy,* which we can apply to this formidable difficulty. How is it met in England, where it must also be a serious obstacle, although not so serious as here—because in England the fall in price measures the whole loss to the producer, but here the fall in price is *aggravated* by the operation of the tariff: e. g., if iron fall in London from £8 to £5, the difference is $15; but here the difference in price is increased by the difference in duty, which at £8 would be $12, while at £5 it is only $7 50-100. When the price falls below the cost of production in England, as during the present year, the great makers stack up their iron, which they are enabled to do from the possession of immense capital, built up at the expense of the whole world, and their own half-paid labour, during periods of high prices. By the strong houses, these extreme depressions are not regarded as *very* serious objections, because it enables them, in the first place, to drive out their weaker competitors; and, secondly, to produce iron at the very cheapest rate, because, then, labour is to be had for mere feeding. As soon as the iron in weak hands has been consumed, the strong houses can dictate their own terms, and dispose of their accumulated stocks at an enormous profit. It is stated on good authority, that Crawshay realized £1,200,000 sterling out of such an operation in 1844!—more money, we can safely assert, than the whole iron business of this country has netted to the iron masters in twenty years.

The natural remedy, then, for these fluctuations, is *adequate capital*, to produce and hold on to stocks, when the price is *lowest*, and to sell when it is *highest*. More money can really be made in this way, than out of a uniform average business, as the maker sells the greater part of his production at the highest price.

No such capital exists in this country; for it is a well-established fact, that notwithstanding the "princely fortunes" we hear of having been realized by iron masters, the capital employed in the business has not, for the last twenty years, yielded seven per cent. interest. This is due to the fact, that no sooner has the iron master been able to get his works into successful operation, and the cost of manufacture reduced to a minimum, than one of the periodical fluctuations comes, which he cannot control, and against which the policy of the government furnishes no security, but tends to aggravate. His works have to suspend, and the skill, to acquire which long years of toil and a fortune have been expended, is dissipated, to be acquired anew, when better prices tempt him to resume. Such a suspension at the Trenton works, for only four months, increased the cost for making rails on a new order, from loss of skill, at least ten dollars per ton.

The difficulty of holding on to the product of an iron establishment, for better prices, is apparent from the fact, that the largest capital devoted to the business in this country, does not exceed a million of dollars, two-thirds of which is fixed capital, in buildings, machinery, &c., while the annual value of the product is equal to the whole capital.

The only resource, then, of the iron master, against these ruinous fluctuations, is in the action of the general government, and here again there is the *most entire harmony* between the interest of the government looking to revenue, and of the producer. We have seen that forty per cent. on the average price, £8, fairly establishes competition between foreign and domestic iron. Now, when iron falls to £5, the foreign maker can take the market, by reason of the fall in price, without reference to the fall in duty. *But the duty does fall*, and the government loses revenue; for iron at £5 can certainly pay the same or even more duty than £8, and still be sold for less money. So when the price of iron advances to £11, the foreign maker, without duty, can but just compete with the domestic producer, and if the duty keeps advancing at the same time, the duty becomes prohibitory—and the government gets no revenue at all.

This whole difficulty is met by a *sliding scale* of duties, as you suggested in your first article. Let the average price, £8, be taken as the basis, and 40 per cent. as the revenue standard, and the iron interest would struggle on, even under the present duty of 30 per cent., if that is decided to be the *revenue* point. For every five shillings sterling fall in the price, let one dollar be added to the duty, and for every advance of five shillings in the price, let one dollar be taken from the duty—and thus the government will always realize the largest possible amount of revenue from iron, and the producer would be secured against being ruined by fluctuations which he cannot control. And when the price of English iron should advance above £12, the consumer would have American iron cheaper than the foreign iron could possibly be procured.

Now, we desire to ask you, whether a duty imposed in this way, does not fulfil all the conditions that can be required of a duty? It is *ad valorem*, and not based upon any fictitious or assumed valuation, (which was the democratic eye-sore in the tariff of 1842); it is strictly a *revenue* duty; it insures to the consumer the *lowest possible average price*, and protects the iron-maker against the only serious impediments in the way of placing his business, with the requisite economy and skill, upon a substantial basis. It meets fully the wants of the government, and is fairly adjusted to the rights of every class in the community. The iron-masters ought not, and do not ask, to have any class taxed for their benefit.

It is frankly admitted, that the consumer has a direct interest in keeping the market open for foreign iron, as a check upon the price of the domestic article. But no reasonable man will urge, that to do this a system should be adopted which aggravates the fluctuations, or that because we import foreign goods, we ought to import at the same time, all the difficulties which have affected the price of these goods, such as Providential dispensations of famine and pestilence; or an uncontrollable spirit of speculation, as developed in the English Railroad mania; or the evils of revolutions resulting from the unjust political systems of Europe. In fact, the whole country is deeply interested, producers and consumers alike, in preventing this land from becoming a "sink" into which shall be emptied all the vials of wrath that are opened on the European world. And yet our present revenue system encourages this very thing. Shall we hesitate to apply the simple remedy, of increasing the duty as the price falls, and diminishing the duty as the price rises, under such judicious regulations as experience has suggested?

We have reached our prescribed limits; but there is still an interesting point, to which, if you can spare us the room, we would advert—and that is, if Congress should make the desired modifications in the duty on iron, is there any prospect that, ultimately, bar-iron can be produced in this country *at a cost not greater* than the average price of bar-iron in Liverpool, £8 or $40 per ton? We have not the slightest hesitation in giving an *affirmative answer*, and the reasons for it.

The cost of making bar-iron in this country, ten years ago, was *fifty per cent.* greater than it is now. Previous to that time, from the want of adequate communication with the interior, iron to be consumed on tide water could only be made with charcoal, and in close proximity to its market. This, as we have seen, is an expensive operation. The first great reduction in cost was only procured by the expenditure of fifty millions of dollars on canals and railroads, by which the ore and mineral coal were made accessible to each other, and to the market on tide water. In 1840, the first anthracite furnace was put into successful operation, and by using the waste heat for making steam and heating the blast, the cost of making pig-iron has been reduced in nine years, to nearly one-half of the cost by the old charcoal process. The next great cheapening of cost resulted from the introduction of anthracite coal in the puddling and reheating process. This was in successful operation in 1844, when the sudden rise in price gave an impetus to the trade, especially in the manufacture of railroad iron, by which the skill of the workmen was perfected. In 1845 the cost of making rails at Trenton was at least $75 per ton. In 1849 it had been reduced to about $50, a reduction of 33⅓ per cent. in four years. This reduction in cost was rapidly progressing, when the ruinously low prices of English iron, produced by famine, speculation, and revolutions, which we could not guard against, compelled the American mills to suspend work, and to lose in a measure the skill acquired by four years of hard work. Under a judicious revenue policy, this skill can soon be regained, but at a heavy loss, and then we shall have only ten dollars more to overcome, to place our cost on a par with the average price of English bars in Liverpool. If $25 have been saved in first cost in four years, is it unreasonable to anticipate a further reduction of ten dollars in as many more? Admitting that the cost of making pig-iron has been brought to a minimum, the rolling mill, where the chief cost is encountered, still remains for improvement. The conversion of coal into gas, and its successful application in that state to puddling and reheating iron, will make a very material saving. The substitution of machinery for some of the manual labour now employed in rolling, would effect another great saving, and this improvement a well-known and most ingenious iron-master in this State is aiming at, with every prospect of success. In fact there never has been a time when so much practical skill and mechanical ingenuity have been turned in this direction. Science, which has hitherto almost neglected, in this country, this ample field for its investigation, is bending its energies to the practical purpose of cheapening iron. All that we need is, an uninterrupted business, so that we can retain and add to our skill, and introduce the improvements which experience and science will dictate.

With such real results achieved, and so little to be done—with such prospects of success, is there not good reason for asking a change in the revenue system, not for the prohibition of foreign competition, but for a change to complete the great work, which American energy has so successfully commenced? England, herself, formerly made iron only with charcoal. This destroyed her ship timber so rapidly, that the use of charcoal was forbidden. But she immediately imposed such a duty on foreign iron, as enabled her iron-masters to enter courageously on the untried task of making iron with mineral coal—and although she has since changed her duties *fifteen* times, it has always been to advance them, till they amounted in 1825 to £7 per ton. By this time her manufacturers had become able to defy the competition of the world, *and not till then was Free Trade in Iron proclaimed.*

What the iron-master wants in this country, is *stability* and not *high duties.* The enactment of a new tariff once a month, would be deprecated by every intelligent man, as ruinous to the best interests of the country. And yet it is against this very difficulty that the iron interest is now struggling—for every change of prices is a change of tariff. Remove this difficulty, either by a *sliding scale* or *specific duties*, or by *restricting the fluctuation of the duties within proper fixed limits*, and the iron interest will cease its complaints. And the change that they desire, is in strict harmony with the wants of the *government*, and the true interests of the *consumer*.

We remain, respectfully,

Your obedient servants,

COOPER & HEWITT.

New York, *December 26th*, 1849.

EXTRACTS FROM A PAPER SUBMITTED BY THE AUTHOR OF THE MEMORIAL.

A Protective Market.

THERE is great misapprehension on the subject of the PROTECTION asked for industry. The term is ill-chosen; because it implies special favour granted to particular branches of manufacture. But it is far from being a mere concern of individuals; it can be shown to be equally a matter of public policy. Suppose the makers of iron in Great Britain and the United States to have equal advantages, and that the manufacture is carried to the utmost extent and the lowest point of remuneration by the home competition in each country; and that the average price in each is the same. If any state of industry could, with advantage, dispense with protection, it would be the case supposed. But it would be clearly the interest of both countries to protect their home markets, even in this case of perfect equality. It would be sound policy to keep the manufacture of an article so important as iron in prime vigour and progress, that the quantity might be increased, and the price reduced by the gradual process of home competition, which, in a protected market, is a severe but sure operation. One of the greatest trials the manufacturers encounter in such cases is, that fluctuation which occurs every few years in all mercantile communities. To bear up under all these, and maintain the full vigour of protection, is a hard trial upon makers of iron, the more so, as in their case their expenses do not admit of being abridged, nor can their manufacture be diminished under a limited demand without heavy loss. Seasons of depression must come in both countries in the case supposed—periods when the markets of each would reject, and be unable to consume the ordinary quantity. It must be thrown somewhere, for neither makers nor merchants are able nor willing to hold the surplus of iron until business recovers its tone and makes its usual demand. If the iron thus remaining on hand in Great Britain is thrown into our markets, it will wholly break them down if firm, and increase and continue the depression if already down. Between the two countries, while prices were up, there would be no transactions in iron, but the conflict would be incessant in periods of depression. It may be safely assumed, however, that without help the manufacturers could never recover from such a conflict; a few years would end the struggle by prostrating a large portion of those engaged. The business would have to be reorganized.

It would be sound policy, therefore, to protect each of these markets from the irregularities of the other. This course is best for the makers of iron, as well as for those who are special consumers, to whom it insures, in the long run, the cheapest supply.

Foreign Iron—Its Influence on Prices.

As every country is dependent mainly on its own industry for its supplies, it is important that the industry which furnishes these supplies should be suitably sustained. The prices of the nine-tenths furnished at home should range at such rates as to keep the production active and increasing. Unless it can be demonstrated that the whole supply could be permanently imported cheaper, it would be suicidal to extinguish the industry on which we are dependent for nine-tenths, in a vain experiment to purchase cheaper elsewhere. The prices in the home market should be such as are made by fair competition in the home market, in which all parties interested can take care of themselves. If our iron is made at home, all the labour which goes into the cost should be adequately compensated; the farmer who furnishes food for man and horse, the manufacturer who furnishes raiment, the labourer and operative who are immediately employed in the production—all these and the consumers must settle the price; the elements are among them, and their combined action must maintain a result the nearest to justice, because they all look to their own interests.

It is unjust and unwise to disturb and change this result by introducing a new element in a supply derived without restriction or regulation from foreign trade. Upon that trade we are not in any sense dependent for pig and bar-iron; we should, indeed, at this time, be makers and consumers of a much larger quantity than we have yet used, if we had not imported a ton of iron the last 20 years. We make the *quantity* we consume, much cheaper than we could import it. Is it just that the tenth of our consumption which we import, should regulate to the injury of the makers of the other nine-tenths, the prices of iron in this country? Yet the price is for the most part controlled by the movements of foreign trade. It happens that our seaports are also the chief markets for distribution of our domestic iron. The prices of every country or district are made at its chief markets. If the consumption of iron on the seaboard is 300,000 tons per annum, the import of 50,000 of foreign iron will control the prices, because it comes in to be sold for what it will bring. It is at once offered below the domestic article, and consumers seeing a disturbing cause in the market, pause until the effect is seen. A pause in the purchase of iron, produces a fall, because some sellers must realize, and buyers take the advantage and keep it. The whole mass of the domestic iron is brought to market to keep pace with consumption, and the price demanded is a remunerating rate, and unless this is obtained the business must perish. The quantity imported is a mere overplus—a remnant from British markets, the sale of which at high or low rates is not a very important or vital matter to the manufacturers who sent it. At most, it is but 10 per cent. of their product, and may be considered as their profit, greater or less, as sold. What is vital to them is their *home price;* if that is fair on the average, they can afford to risk 10 per cent. of their production in our market. Let any one who knows how prices are made to vary, not only by actual events, but by rumours and suspicions, reflect upon the effect of an additional 10 per cent. of a foreign article thrown in upon a previously balanced market, and he will perceive not only the necessary depression but the injustice of it to the industry affected.

But there is a feature in foreign trade which greatly increases the mischief of leaving the market under its control. It is to a most extraordinary degree uncertain and fluctuating. The importing merchants are governed in some degree, doubtless, by the actual demand, and their imports might, if exhibited, separately show some regularity. But a large portion of the imports are sent upon speculation, and the quantity depends on markets abroad and the thousand contingencies which may determine a larger or less export to our shores. The irregularity of our imports of iron from Great Britain is so striking as to demonstrate the impolicy and injustice of making the prices of the domestic product subservient to it. Beginning with the year 1820, coming down to 1845, and leaving out the fractional hundreds, the following figures exhibit the number of thousands of tons of iron of all kinds imported into the United States from Great Britain each year in its order:

Year.	Tons.	Year.	Tons.	Year.	Tons.
1820,	8,000	1830,	21,000	1840,	72,000
1821,	9,000	1831,	41,000	1841,	112,000
1822,	15,000	1832,	45,000	1842,	107,000
1823,	13,000	1833,	62,000	1843,	38,000
1824,	11,000	1834,	47,000	1844,	102,000
1825,	13,000	1835,	63,000	1845,	68,000
1826,	12,000	1836,	91,000	1846,	——
1827,	21,000	1837,	54,000	1847,	——
1828,	22,000	1838,	78,000	1848,	——
1829	17,000	1839,	85,000	1849,	315,000

These figures show a variation in the supply of iron derived from Great Britain of from 10 to upwards of 200 per cent., between one year and the next. Small as this quantity appears, compared with our whole consumption, it would always control the prices in New York, and thence those in the country. How little these fits and starts of commerce are like the sober pursuits of industry at home, where the annual product only varies to increase with the gradual increase of labour, capital, and consumption.

How can it be just to make the labourer's wages depend upon the variable movements of foreign trade?

Manufacture of Iron.

We cannot manufacture iron in the United States as cheaply as it is made in Great Britain. Because:—

1. The erection of furnaces and machinery costs from a third to a half less there. Iron enters largely into these constructions. The wages of all mechanics are not more than half our rates.

2. The wages of the operators in iron works are about half that which is paid here.

3. The cheapness of money there has enabled the manufacturers to prosecute their business with more vigour and more economy; and to introduce at once many modes of saving expense, the cost of which cannot be reached by makers here.

4. The manufacture in its present improved processes has many years the start there. We might, and, with our home market secured to us, could soon equal them in all departments, as we do in many now.

If we could import and pay for our whole supply at the low rates, it would be more difficult to refute the advocates of the cheap market. The iron market in Great Britain affords a spectacle of fluctuation and speculation which has scarce any parallel. The range of prices varies from below the cost of manufacture to 150 per cent. advance upon the actual cost. It has been with British manufactures, for the last twenty years, a constantly recurring feast or famine. Iron being an article not subject to deterioration, it is deemed safe to hold, and speculators step in when prices are at the lowest. Not only so, but at extremely low rates iron enters into a large consumption for which it is too expensive at higher rates. At the low rates this increased consumption begins; contracts are made, enterprises are commenced, plans and estimates are gone into, which produce at last an effective demand for iron sufficient to enable makers and holders to advance the rates in proportion to the wants of buyers, who hasten to supply themselves when the advance begins.

These fluctuations in price cannot be wondered at if we note the progress of the manufacture. The following is the estimate of the quantity produced in the years named:

Year.	Tons.	Exported to all the world. Tons.	Consumed.
1810,	294,642		
1820,	368,000	91,766	276,234
1825,	581,367	69,328	
1830,	678,417	130,417	
1835,	1,000,000	219,203	
1840,	1,500,000	268,328	1,231,672

The increase in product in 30 years was over 500 per cent.* The increase in the export was less than 300 per cent. The increased consumption was very nearly 500 per cent. There was in that period no parallel to this progress in the world. It is not hard to comprehend the share which this increased consumption of iron had in the *material progress* of Great Britain.

If this manufacture is not overdone in Great Britain, it would be difficult to find any business overdone. It is only possible to keep up this large production through the operation of those fluctuations, by which, in times of depression, the iron is taken into a large consumption at the low rates, and by which the makers indemnify themselves for the losses of one period by the high prices of another. By this system they export largely when they can do no better, and raise the prices so high at times, that exports must be greatly diminished. Upon this system of variation, the makers there thrive; but can these fluctuations be introduced elsewhere with advantage, or even without ruin?

* The increase in 50 years was 100 per cent.

They are an incident to over-production there—they are an incalculable injury when brought to bear upon our industry.

Protection of Prices.

As the progress of the manufacture of iron in Great Britain is one of the greatest achievements of industry in modern times, it may be worth while to consider what protection fostered and secured this wonderful growth.

Previous to this growth, pig-iron had been scarcely known in commerce. England had no rival in the production of that article that could disturb her markets. The price may be shown thus:

Period	Years	Price	Average
1782 to 1803	20 years,	£3 to £9	Average £6.
1803 to 1818	15 years,	£7 to £9	Average £8.
1818 to 1840	22 years,	£4 15 to £11	Average £6.
1840 to 1849	9 years,	£2 to £5	Average £3 5.

It will be seen that down to the year 1840 from 1782, in which period the production of iron in Great Britain had increased from 150,000 tons to 1,500,000 or ten fold, the makers enjoyed a price averaging over £6, and very seldom below £5. Upon this price the business flourished beyond precedent. After 1840, it became evident that there was an over-production, and the British market broke down. The price of Scotch pig, which, after 1840, controlled the market, fell to £2, and even below that rate. It became the subject of speculation and fluctuation beyond any article of commerce.

It was the protection of this continued high price, for 50 years which stimulated the production of pig-iron. The revenue duty of 27½ per cent., was of no consequence; the importations of pig-iron were too small to have any effect upon the markets.

Large importations of bar-iron were made into Great Britain between 1782 and 1840; but that it may be clearly seen how far this importation interfered with the domestic product, note the prices of Russian and Swedish bars, the only kinds largely imported.

Russian bars.	1782 1795	13 years, from	£10 15 16	Average £16.
Do.	1795 1803	8 years,	£17 25	Average 21.
Do.	1803 1820	17 years,	£12 10 22	Average 16.
Do.	1820 1840	20 years,	£14 26	Average 19.
Do.	1840 1849	9 years,		Average 16.

Swedish Bars.	1782 1795	from	£14 15 18	Average £16.
Do.	1795 1803	from	£19 26	Av'ge £22 10.
Do.	1803 1820	from	£15 10 21	Average £17.
	Since 1820 the average has been about			£13.

The above prices are exclusive of duty, which was increased from £2 16s 6d in 1782, by *ten different advances,* to £6 10, (and £7 18s 6d. in foreign ships,) in 1820.

These prices were indeed in no degree an obstacle to the British manufacturers; they were, in fact, so high that no heavy importations could take place.

The largest importation in any year between 1800 and 1814 of bar iron, was 52,873 tons in 1802; during the nine years of that period the importation did not reach 30,000, and was sometimes below 20,000 tons.

From 1815 to 1840, the largest quantity of bar iron imported into Great Britain, was 25,033 tons in 1836, but the average for the whole period was considerably below 20,000 tons.

The British manufacturers required no legislative aid after 1800, yet such caution was used that the duties were increased from time to time to 1820, and were not removed until 1825.

PROTECTION IN UNITED STATES BY PRICES.

The British maker had competitors who furnished iron exclusive of duty at from $65 to $100 per ton.

The competitor of our manufacturers has furnished bar iron

From 1815 to 1830 at $50	highest $72. lowest $31.
From 1830 to 1849 at $38	highest $55. lowest $22.

But low as the averages are, compared with those against which the British manufacturer had to contend, they afford an inadequate idea of the destructive effect of this competition. The averages are comparatively high from the excessive range of the fluctuation. For three years from June 1820, to July 1824, the price did not exceed $46, and did not average over $42.

From March, 1827, to July, 1836, the price did not exceed $46.

From April, 1829, to October, 1835, the price did not exceed $37.

From March, 1830, to March, 1833, the price did not exceed $33, and for a year of this period it was under $27.

For three years, including 1841 to 1843, the price was at $24, and during 1842 as low as $22.

It is such prolonged depressions as these which seriously injure, if they do not ruin, the maker of iron in the United States. He cannot meet such exigencies, neither by reduction of his expenditures, by reducing wages, nor by diminishing the amount of his product. He must continue his business at a serious loss for years, or he must stop and be ruined.

It cannot be doubted that these periods of low prices have hindered the progress of this branch of industry to a very important extent. It is scarcely extravagant to say that with the same comparative protection which has been enjoyed in Great Britain, the product here would now have been scarce less than that of that country. If the home market had been equally secure to the makers here, as that of Great Britain was to the makers there, the consumption of iron here might now be 1,500,000 tons. The higher price would have been no obstacle, for where all labour receives a corresponding compensation, the price is no obstacle in the exchange of labour. These fluctuations in prices, introduced from Great Britain, have proved an incalculable evil to the whole industry of the country. The fact that a portion of our annual supply has been imported at a very low cost, much lower than it could be produced for here, is no alleviation. Instead of consuming more, we have consumed less. Our consumers say that they work up far less iron at the low rates than when business is proceeding on the basis of home prices.

If owing to the low prices of British iron we consume 200,000 tons less of domestic iron, we prevent the circulation of a value of $10,000,000, which, at $50 as the average per ton of pig and bar, would be its cost in food, labour, clothing, &c. All who are concerned in this great exchange are thrown out of their usual routine of employment.—The farmer loses his market—the labourer his wages—the manufacturer his living—all are made less able to consume, and of course others who are dependent on them feel and suffer by the change, until the $10,000,000, by endless ramifications of the channels in which its benefits would have been felt, becomes hundreds of millions in its consequences. The effect of stopping the domestic manufacture is to throw business entirely out of the usual channels. It is too absurd to be held by any one, that the elements which would go to make 200,000 tons of iron in the United States, could be made available to import that quantity and pay for it. If imported, it must be paid for in something else than *iron ore, coal, wood, veal, mutton, potatoes, turnips, oats, rye, corn, and American labour.*

Free Trade.

It is a strange feature of Free Trade doctrines, that while they regard commerce as the great patron and regulator of industry, they wholly omit to make any allowance for the effect of commercial movement upon prices. The ability to make goods cheaply implies, with them, a willingness to sell them cheaply, without change of price. If all taxes, duties, and restraints were removed from commerce, the advocates of free trade seem to think the very facility of movement and transportation would furnish all the stimulus industry requires. They omit all notice of the fact that merchants, to whose tender mercies the producing classes are invited to commit themselves, are as much addicted to habits of thrift as other people; and that prices fluctuate more by these movements, and are more influenced by their operations, than by the efforts of producers. Merchants, in proportion to their number, are far better paid than manufacturers, and when the latter are starving, the former are often making large profits. It is quite as acceptable to the merchant to make a large profit on a few goods, as a small one upon many. The interest of the producing classes is to furnish a large product and a large exchange that the comforts, luxuries, and benefits of mutual industry may be extended to the largest number. It is their interest to reduce commercial power and influence to its just minimum, because it is a charge upon industry. All the profits of the merchant are laid upon the consumer, and proportionably reduce the ability of the consumer to increase his consumption, and thereby make a large demand upon the producer. The truth is, that merchants have grasped a power and wield it for their own benefit, which enables them to oppress both producer and consumer. However necessary this may be, the merchants are certainly not the appropriate patrons of industry; they, as shrewd men usually do, take care of themselves, and whether trade is free or not, no men can be in a better position to keep guard over their own interests. They survey the whole field of trade: occupying an intermediate post between consumer and producer, it is their interest to buy as cheaply as possible and sell as dearly. It is at their instigation that the doctrines of free trade are so loudly proclaimed. They and their friends are no doubt sincere. There is one great fact, however, which cannot be explained upon their principles—that industry, widely diffused industry, manufacturing industry upon the mighty scale now seen in Europe and the United States, has grown up under the protection of commercial restrictions. The productive powers of man were never exhibited before the days of the protective duties as they have been since. Commerce was free when Tyre, Carthage, the Grecian cities, Alexandria, Venice, Genoa, the Hanse towns, Holland, at their several periods of prosperity usurped the trade of the world. The merchants were then all in all—the merchants were princes, the producers slaves. Free trade would rapidly tend to the same results now.

If the question related solely to the prosperity of trade, there might be force in the position, that men in trade should be allowed to take care of themselves. The problem for solution is not what will most promote the interests of those engaged in commerce, but what will best promote the interests of all.

So far from being that department of industry which most requires the care of government, or rather best deserves to have its wishes granted, commerce is really a tax, an incumbrance upon industry, to be reduced as far as practicable. It is the expense incurred in distribution—an expense which, like all other mere expenses, should be kept at the lowest point consistent with the end in view.

What then will most promote the comfort and material well-being of the mass of the people? We reply, that industry which furnishes the largest product for the consumption of the masses, whilst all the producers receive, by a fair exchange for their labour, their full share of those articles which minister to comfort and physical well-being: —that industry, which, while it is thus successful in securing physical benefits, has a surplus large enough to maintain a good and efficient government, and all the advantages and enjoyments which belong to education, morality, philanthropy, and religion. Are these benefits to be obtained by merely removing restraints from the plans and movements of men in trade? This is no more true nor wise than to say that there should be no *checks or locks* upon the wheels which carry the goods to market.

We must inquire what are the circumstances, in which men will and can exert their utmost productive powers. Clearly, where they consider their compensation most secure, and where the division of labour can at once, and in the same locality, be carried to such a point that a large exchange of labour can be effected, free from the expenses of transportation and intervening profits. Producers being consumers, and these being also producers, that is their best business which is done most directly, because it is that in which they are most likely to obtain mutual compensation in the results of their mutual labour. In all large manufacturing operations, one of the first considerations entertained by those who contemplate such undertakings, is, the facility of selling the products in such quantities as may enable the manufacturer to sustain his business at the low prices to which competition may force his sales. The ready sale of the product is vital to the business, even if the profits are reduced to zero. The annual expenses of a blast furnace are from $200 to $300 each day, an expenditure which will rapidly absorb the working capital of its owner, if not replenished by corresponding sales. In many of the iron establishments of this country the daily outlay is equal to, and in some, over $2000. A regular market is, therefore, indispensable. The manufacturer may estimate with reasonable correctness the demand and the competition of the home market, but must be wholly at fault in conjecturing what interference may come from abroad. He knows that his market at home may be disturbed, and, for a time, destroyed by any undue ingress of the foreign article; for experience has taught him that his sales are at an end for a time, when a cheaper article appears. When this happens, buyers become "bears, and operate for a decline," and this they effect by ceasing further purchases, until the market finds its lowest point,—that is, until the necessities of the manufacturer compel him to come to the terms of the buyers.

Necessity of a Home Market.

The necessity of securing the home market to the home producer may be thus stated. A manufacturer has observed that his country has, for a long period, been supplied with a certain article at a range of prices at which he thinks he could furnish it. He consults the consumers of the article, and they encourage him to go on, agreeing to give him the preference. He makes a large outlay, and begins his work. His goods go off freely, and he has the market. The foreign article must now be withdrawn or reduced in price; it cannot be withdrawn, for there is no other market, and the price is reduced. The home producer is now receiving his first lesson, and he must reduce his rates also, at the first stage of his operations; the foreigner only after a long period of success. It becomes now a struggle for existence, the foreigner having the accumulated wealth of a long career, determines to extinguish his young rival, and again reduces the price. The home producer applies to the government for protection, and though the whole array of free trade arguments are brought to bear against the application, it prevails, and a specific duty is laid which gives the producer a price at which he can maintain his production in full vigour. The foreigner, determined still to conquer the market, reduces his price according to the duty, or in other words, pays the duty and enters the lists again. At this stage of the struggle, the whole quiver of free trade weapons are let loose upon the monopolist, who is charged with receiving a premium to the whole amount of the duty, to sustain a manufacture that ought never to have been started. The absurdity of not buying altogether in this cheap market, strikes the philosophers of the closet so strongly, that they cannot express their surprise at the dull intellects of mere men of business. To resume our case:—the home producer is again forced to ask further protection, and to say that his business must perish if he does not obtain it. Again, common sense prevails over theory, a heavier duty is laid, and his business revives, though suffering severely from these interruptions, and by no means in the state of efficiency it would have been but for their influence. If it be supposed that the foreigner is unable to continue the struggle unaided, he applies next to his government for the removal of certain taxes, charges, duties, which bear upon his products, for the avowed object of enabling him to retain the foreign market, of which he is deprived.

Thus may a struggle be carried on for many years, to the serious injury of both parties—perhaps to their ruin. The operatives engaged in the home product, thus injured, must suffer severely; while the advocates of free trade cry out "let them fight it out," the merchants, who are the real purchasers, find their interests greatly promoted by the contest, as the lion's share falls to them.

It is thus, too, that the cheapness of a foreign market, which makes it the very climax of free trade arguments, is caused by want of demand for its goods; that want of demand arises from home production, which deprives the cheap market of their customers. The more the foreign market is thus cheapened by home production, the more the necessity is increased to afford protection to that market, on which the home production is mainly dependent. Individual merchants and consumers are always prompt enough to avail themselves of a cheap market when it offers; but nations should never commit their people to the absurdity of relying upon any market because it is cheap. The policy of a nation cannot be changed with the productions of a market, but it is the business of individuals to watch the market and operate wherever advantage calls them. The United States cannot obtain her whole supply of iron from Great Britain in one quarter of the year, make it at home the next, and go abroad for it the next:—nor can this be done if the quarters are extended to years, or to periods of five years.

It is worthy of remark, that while free trade theorists cry out *laissez faire*, as summing up all the wisdom needed by governments in the management of trade, they stop the mouths of labourers, artisans, and manufacturers, as not knowing, or not to be trusted with their own interests. Who are to be "*let alone?*"—the merchants. These agents, these buyers, transporters, and sellers of the products of industry ask, by their friends of the free trade philosophy, to have the whole business committed to them—to be *let alone*—while they exert every faculty, every nerve, and all the shrewdness, superior knowledge and address they possess, under the stimulus of all the selfishness of human nature in the prospect of gain, for their own benefit. But let it be noted that the producers and the manufacturer do not cry "*let us alone*"—their cry in Europe for the last century and more has been for *protection*, and it has been accorded. Under this protection the products of Europe have increased at a rate five-fold the increase of population. But this *let us alone* policy is put forth only in behalf of the foreign merchants; the merchant of the domestic products unites with his special patrons. The foreign merchant, whose business represents but a tithe of the business of the country, asks to have the interest of the nine-tenths committed to him. This cannot be denied; let the manifestos of free trade be examined, and it will be found that they mock at the manufacturer, scoff at his statements, complaints and petitions. It has been so for a century; yet the doctrine of protection has been in the main the policy of every modern civilized nation during that period, in which industry and the arts has made more progress in one century than in thousands of years before. It is true, that in England, and in some other countries, some departments of industry have been so long and so fully protected, that with the advantage of cheap labour and cheap capital, they no longer require *protection;* and the persons interested in these branches of production may now join in the cry of free trade, as they naturally wish to remove all obstacles to carrying their goods to all the markets of the world. These exceptions only prove their rule; they are exceptions only because the rule existed. Let manufacturers, small and great, then be heard, not only in their defence, but permit them to state what is required for their security and their success; let them be heard and regarded as representing the producing classes, the industry of the country.

The following Certificates have been placed in the hands of the Committee for Publication.

The undersigned, machinists and consumers of iron, but in no manner engaged in the manufacture thereof, resident in Philadelphia and the vicinity, certify that we do not find the low price of foreign Iron any advantage in our general business. In many instances, the consumption of our manufactures has greatly diminished, and in others the stagnation which prevails, when any great interest, like that of the manufacture of iron, is suffering, extends to others, checks demand and clogs all the operations of business, until all suffer like injury. We find consumption greatest, and business most satisfactory, when remunerating prices are general, and when all branches of business are in full activity.

Neall & Matthews, Bush Hill Machine Shop and Foundry.
James T. Sutton & Co., Franklin Iron Works, Kensington.
Thomas B. Chapman, Soho Work, Kensington.

T. & B. Rowland, Shovel Manufacturers.

Savery & Co., Cast Iron Hollow Ware Foundry.

Arundius Tiers, Point Pleasant Foundry.

Reaney, Neafie & Co., Penn Steam Engine and Boiler Works.

Boston, January 31st, 1850.

To the Committee on the Iron Memorial, Philadelphia:

Gentlemen:—

In reply to your inquiries, we say that in our experience, we find no corresponding advantage in our general business from low prices of foreign iron.

We are large consumers of Pig Iron, and although now able to purchase our raw material from 20 to 30 per cent. cheaper than in 1846, our business is less profitable, because greatly diminished. The consumption of our manufactured articles falls off, when the manufacture of iron languishes, and orders fail us when foreign iron is plenty and cheap.

	Melt per annum.
Cyrus Alger & Co., - - - -	5000 tons.
Charles S. Storrow, - - - -	2500 tons.
James K. Mills & Co., - - -	2500 tons.
William Amory, - - - -	2500 tons.
G. M. Palmer, - - - - -	500 tons.
Wm. Thomas & Co., - - - -	3000 tons.
Williams, Bird & Co., - - -	2500 tons.
B. T. Reed, Sr., - - - - -	5000 tons.
R. P. Davis, - - - - -	1000 tons.

BOSTON, January 2, 1850.

SIR:—

I can easily answer your inquiries as to the present condition of the Iron manufacture in this State. The business is at end. Of the three large rolling-mills here, two have stopped, and the third is preparing to stop. One of them has just been sold at auction for about the value of the land and houses, and the machinery taken as old iron. Of the eight charcoal furnaces in the western part of the State, that were in blast in 1846, not one, I believe, is now at work. If the present state of things is to last, the capital invested in these works is lost, and the peculiar skill and knowledge the workmen have acquired—their capital—is equally wasted.

I do not think the iron-masters here wish for prohibitory duties or extravagantly high ones; but they certainly do hope that the duty, whatever it is, may be made specific, that we may know what to depend upon. The duty on refined iron in 1847, was $16 00, and less than $10 00 in 1849. We have as much skill in the business here, probably, as the English iron-masters have. We have all their processes with our own improvements; and in addition there have been many useful inventions introduced here from Germany and France. But we have not such large capitals. They can sustain themselves under losing prices much longer than we can. And now that they are aided by our ad valorem duty, that gives us protection when we do not need it, and withdraws it when we do, they might ruin every iron manufacturer in New England, without, after all, selling their iron here any lower than we could afford to, *taking a series of years together.*

Your ob't serv't,

CHARLES JACKSON, JR.

(From the Plough, Loom and Anvil.)

THE HARMONY OF INTERESTS.

BY H. C. CAREY.

Domestic Production of Iron.

In 1810, the whole number of furnaces in the Union was 153, yielding 54,000 tons of metal, equal to 16 pounds per head of the population.

1821, the manufacture was in a state of ruin.

1828, the product had reached 130,000 tons, having little more than doubled in eighteen years.

1829, it was 142,000. Increase in one year, nearly ten per cent.

1830, it was 165,000. Increase in two years, more than twenty-five per cent.

1831, it was 191,000. Increase in three years about 50 per cent.

1832, it was 200,000, giving an increase in three years of above sixty per cent.

1840, the quantity given by the census was 286,000, but a committee of the Home League, in New York, made it 347,700 tons. Taking the medium of the two, it would give about 315,000 tons, being an increase in 8 years of 50 per cent.

1842, a large portion of the furnaces were closed, and the product had fallen to probably little more than 200,000, but certainly less than 230,000 tons.

1846, it was estimated, by the Secretary of the Treasury, at 765,000 tons, having trebled in four years.

1847, it was supposed to have reached the amount of not less than 800,000 tons.

1848, it became stationary.

1849, many furnaces being already closed, the production of the present year cannot be estimated above 650,000 tons; but from the accumulation of stock and the difficulty of selling it, it is obvious that the diminution will be greater.

Communication from Samuel J. Reeves to the General Committee, on the Elementary Cost of making Pig and Bar Iron.

A.

Elementary Cost of making a ton of Pig Iron on the Schuylkill River, at the Furnaces situated between Norristown and Spring Mills.

DATA.

$2\frac{2}{3}$ tons of iron ore delivered at furnace,	at $2 00 per ton,		$5 33
2 " of coal in the furnace, $\frac{1}{4}$ " extra for steam, smith fires, &c.,	$2\frac{1}{4}$ at 3 25 "		7 31
1 " limestone,	at 75 "		75
			13 39
Furnace labour,		2 00	
Other expenses, labour, wear and tear, superintendence, interest, &c.,		2 11	4 11
			$17 50

IRON ORE.

	Labour.	Other items.			
Ore leave,		40 cts. per ton, at $2\frac{2}{3}$ tons,		1 06	
Mining,	1 00		"		2 67
Hauling,	50		"		1 33
Weighing, &c.	10		"		27
	1 60 +	40		1 06 +	4 27=5 33

COAL.

	Labour.	Other items.			
Rent,		35 cts. at $2\frac{1}{4}$ tons,		$78\frac{3}{4}$	
Operator's profit,		18 "	"	$40\frac{1}{2}$	
Mining,	90 cts.		"		2 $02\frac{1}{2}$
Charges on lateral roads, at 25 cts.,	13 "	12 "	"	27	$29\frac{1}{4}$
Wear and tear, 15 cts.,	12 "	3 "	"	$6\frac{3}{4}$	27
Incidental labour,	7 "		"		$15\frac{3}{4}$
Reading railroad, 1 30,	70 "	60 "	"	1 35	1 $57\frac{1}{2}$
Interest,		5 "	"	$11\frac{1}{4}$	
	1 92	1 33		2 99+	4 32 = 7 31

LIMESTONE.

	Labour.	Other items.					
Quarry leave,		10 cts. at 1 ton,	10				
Quarrying,	25				25		
Hauling,	40				40		
	65	10	10	+	65	=	75

GENERAL EXPENSES.

	Labour.		Other items.		
Furnace labour,	2 00				
Other labour and expenses,	1 11	+	1 00		
Total general expenses,	3 11	+	1 00	=	$4 11
Forward Ore,	4 27	+	1 06	=	5 33
" Coal,	4 32	+	2 99	=	7 31
" Limestone,	65	+	10	=	75
	12 35	+	5 15	=	17 50

The above shows the amount of labour represented by a ton of pig iron to be $12 35, and the amount of other items, not labour, composed of profits paid for the privilege of mining the minerals, coal operators' profits, and interest on investments, &c., to be $5 15.

Every anthracite furnace thus situated, making 5000 tons of metal per annum, will benefit the following interests thus:

Clear profits to the Reading and other lateral railroads,* for transporting coal to furnace,	1 62	$8,100
Rent to owners of coal lands,	78½	3,925
Profit to the coal operators,	40½	2,025
Ore leave to owners of ore lands,	1 06	5,300
Quarry leave to owners of limestone quarries,	10	500
Capitalists and storekeepers,	1 18	5,900
	5 15	25,750
Labourers engaged in mining and transporting, &c., and about the works,	12 35	61,750
	17 50	87,500
Transportation to market, 75; and drayage, 50,	1 25	} 12,500
Selling and guarantee commission, 5 per cent.,	1 00	
Storage, weighing, &c.,	25	
5000 tons pig iron cost when sold,	20 00	100,000
5000 tons sold at present market price,	20 00	100,000
Profit to the manufacturer,	00	00

B.

Analysis of the cost of Merchant Bar Iron manufactured on the Schuylkill River, from Pig Iron costing $17 50 *at the Mill.*

DATA.

1⅓ tons of pig-iron, at $17 50, - - - -	$23 38
2¼ tons of coal, at 3 25, - - - -	7 31
Labour per ton, - - - - - - -	15 00
Interest, $1 00; wear and tear, $1 00; general expenses, $1 31,	3 31
	$49 00

INTERESTS BENEFITED.

	By Furnace.	By Rolling Mill.	Total.
Stockholders of Reading and lateral roads, clear profits for carrying coal, in making 1⅓ tons pig-iron, and in making one ton of bars,	2 16	1 62	3 78
Rent to owners of coal lands,	1 04½	79	1 83½
Profit to coal operators,	54	41	95
Ore leave to owners of ore lands,	1 41⅓		1 41⅓
Quarry leave to owners of limestone lands,	13⅓		13⅓
Capitalists and storekeepers,	1 57⅓	2 31	3 88⅓
	6 87 +	5 13 =	12 00

LABOUR.

Coal miners and labourers, - -	3 66	2 75	6 41
Labour for transporting coal, - -	2 10	1 79½	3 89½
Mining, hauling, &c., - - -	5 69		5 69
Quarrying and delivering limestone,	87		87
Furnace labour, - - - - -	4 14		4 14
Mill labour, $15, and wear and tear, $1		16 00	16 00
	16 46 +	20 54 =	37 00
Brought down, - - - - - - - -			12 00
			49 00
Add transportation to market,	1 00		
Porterage, &c.,	50		
Com. and guarantee, 5 per ct. on $55,	2 75		
Charges,	50		4 75
			53 75
Cr. by sales at $55 per ton, - - - - - - -			55 00
Profit to manufacturer, - - - - - - - -			$1 25

Every complete establishment producing 10,000 tons of merchant bars per annum, pays to diversified labour, at - -	$37 00	per ton,	$370,000
To the owners of coal in the ground, at	1 83½	"	18,350
To the coal operator, clear profit, at	95	"	9,500
To the owners of ore lands, for ore leave, at	1 41	"	14,100
To the owners of limestone quarries, for quarry leave, at - - - - -	13⅓	"	1,333
To capitalists, for the use of money, interest, &c., at - - - - - -	1 50	"	15,000
To Railroad and Canal companies, clear profits over and above expenses, for carrying coal to works, at - - -	3 78	"	37,800
To storekeepers and others, for merchandise, &c., oil, brass, fire-brick, &c., at	2 39⅙	"	23,917
Cost at works, at - - - - - -	49 00	"	490,000
Transportation to market, say at - -	1 00	"	10,000
Drayage and hauling, at - - - -	50	"	5,000
Storage and other expenses, at - -	50	"	5,000
Commission for selling and guarantee, at 5 per cent., - - - - - -	2 75	"	27,500
	53 75	"	537,500
Cr. by sales at market price, at - -	55 00	"	550,000
Profit to manufacturer, at - - - -	1 25	"	12,500

Such is the catalogue of interests benefited by the manufacturer of iron; among which he distributes $537,500 in making 10,000 tons of bars, whether he derives any profit from his business or not. Is he not, therefore, emphatically wasting his time, money and experience for the benefit of the public? To do this amount of business, his capital invested in buildings, machinery, and ready cash, must amount to $500,000; for which, on the supposition that he can sell his iron for $55 per ton, which is above the present market rates, he realizes about 2½ per cent. per annum. Such is the compensation he now receives, if indeed any, for keeping in motion a branch of industry which employs more labour, and disburses more money through the ramified channels of trade, than any other—actually creating capital which otherwise would never exist.

When his works are in operation, he supports, directly and indirectly, more than 1200 men, with their families, in all, not less than 6000 people; whose aggregate earnings we have shown to amount to $370,000 per annum. When such an establishment is closed by British competition, the means of living to these 6000 people are suddenly cut off. Does any one, then, seriously assert that the labouring man and his family are not benefited by protection? The advocates of free trade, nevertheless, do not cease to tell them, either ignorantly or designedly, that it is the manufacturers only, as a class, who are benefited.

The owners of coal lands in Schuylkill County, many of whom live out of the region, and are engaged in other occupations, derive an income of $1 83 per ton, on every ton of bar-iron made; but when the works cease operating this income is at an end.

The coal operator also has a direct profit in every ton of bar-iron made, to the extent of near one dollar per ton. The owners of ore lands and limestone quarries, who are in most instances farmers, may cultivate their fields, and raise vegetables for supplying the wants of the workmen, at the highest market rates, without the necessity of losing time and money in going to the city, and at the same time receive $1 56, from the iron manufacturer, on every ton of bars made, for the privilege alone of digging the ore and quarrying the limestone, which, but for the iron works, would be utterly worthless. These advantages, however, result only when the works are in blast, for when Free Trade puts out the fires, neither ore nor limestone are wanted, nor can the farmers sell their grain and vegetables to the workmen, whose ability to purchase departs with their occupation.

The clear profit to the Railroad and Canal Companies in carrying the one article of coal from the mines to the works, is $3 78 per ton of bars made, and when such an establishment, situated on the line of these improvements, stops for a year, the loss to the stockholders and bondholders of these improvements, amounts to $37,800 per annum. Besides coal, there is an additional profit in transporting other raw materials, miscellaneous articles, the manufactured iron, and passengers to and from the works.

Again, the capitalist and owners of bank stock, who discount the business paper of the manufacturer, pocket $1 50 for every ton of bars made.

Besides the above named, the draymen and the labourers along the wharves derive a benefit, and last of all, the commission merchant is sure to secure a handsome living out of the enterprise of the manufacturer.

All these vast interests are secured in their profits, before the manufacturer can receive a dollar for himself. Are they not all then as much interested in the success of the business as he?

Not less than forty millions of dollars are paid out every year in this manner to the public, through the operations of all the iron works in the United States, when the business is prosperous. With what truth can it be said then, that protection is a tax upon the many for the benefit of the few? It is true that iron, at the present time, is furnished at low prices by Great Britain, but let the home manufacture be destroyed, and it will immediately be dear again. It cannot be doubted, that if all the iron works in the United States should be closed for only one year, and we should depend upon England for our entire supplies, British bar-iron would bring $100 per ton in New York, in less than six months, and the country at the end of the year would be bankrupt, by the drain of $40,000,000 of specie, to pay for it.

"But," say the advocates of Free Trade, "not so, we would pay for it by the exportation of our breadstuffs."

Let us see.

Political economists usually allow, for each individual in this country, a consumption of the products of the land to the value of $50 per annum. The number of people supported by the iron business of the whole country, is *ab ovo usque ad malum* about 600,000, who at $50 per head, consume annually $30,000,000 worth of breadstuffs. If these cannot find employment in manufacturing, they must become producers, and thus is a home market to this immense amount lost to the present producers.

The total exports of breadstuffs from this country to all the world, for the year ending December 24th, 1849, amounted to only $22,895,783, of which Great Britain and Ireland took $14,157,666, not equal in value to the iron we imported from that country last year. Thus it would appear, that the iron business furnishes a larger market to the farmer at home, and at better prices than all the world beside. And furthermore, that Great Britain, which offers to make all our iron and everything else, takes less than the moiety of the farmers' products consumed by the iron manufacturer at his side.

Instead, then, of discouraging the progress of the home manufacture of iron, as the advocates of Free Trade propose to do, for the avowed benefit of the farmers, no policy having this tendency could be devised more injurious to the great agricultural interest. On the contrary, that policy would be the best for the producers of this country, which would tend to double the present home manufacture of iron;—in accomplishing which, they would at once make 600,000 new customers entirely dependent upon them for $30,000,000 of breadstuffs, which is more than the boasted market of the world took from them last year.

Every complete iron works, capable of producing 10,000 tons of bar iron per annum, supports, as we have said before, 6000 people, and makes a market to the farmers in the sphere of its influence, to the extent of $300,000 per annum. Suppose 1000 farmers to participate equally in the advantages of this market, supplying beef, mutton, pork, butter, eggs, vegetables, etc., this will give to each ready sales to the extent of $300, one half of which will be for perishable produce that will not bear exportation.

"But," says the opponent of protection, "it is unjust to tax the farmer for the iron used in making his hoes, harrows, ploughs, axes, &c."

Let us see what this tax amounts to among these 1000 farmers. One thousand pounds per annum is a large allowance for the average consumption of iron among farmers; this is sold to the blacksmiths, wheelwrights, and makers of hoes and harrows, by the manufacturers at, say three cts. per lb., which is $30 for each. Beyond this the farmer is not interested in the enhanced prices caused by a protective duty on iron, because the main cost of his agricultural implements is made up of the additional labour put upon them. Now if the duty is added to the price, assuming it to be at the rate of $17 per ton, 1000 lbs. would pay a duty of $7 60, which, deducted from $30, would, if sold at cost of importation, make the foreign article worth $22 40. This difference, then, of $7 50, is the utmost possible injury the farmer can sustain: while in compensation for this, if he can only supply all the workmen engaged in getting the materials, transporting and manufacturing but 10 tons of bar iron per annum, he will sell them $300 worth of pork, butter, eggs, vegetables, and other products of the farm, besides making a market for his limestone, iron ore, lumber, and many other articles necessary in the construction and operation of an iron works. The loss to the farmer in time alone, not to speak of other expenses, in disposing of $300 worth of produce in a distant market, far exceeds the nominal tax he is supposed to pay for preserving a never-failing and invaluable home market, such as the iron manufacturer affords him.

If we resolve our importations of iron and manufactures of iron and steel into their original elements of cost, we shall find that in this shape we have been large importers of British breadstuffs, coal, iron ore, limestone, labour, &c.

Let us examine into this matter.

The imports into the United States from Great Britain for the fiscal year ending June 30, 1849, were as follows:

Bar iron,	173,473	tons, value,	$6,060,068
Hammered iron,	10,595	"	525,770
Hoops and sheets,	11,174	"	543,256
	195,245		7,129,094
Pig iron,	105,632	"	1,405,613
Steel,	6,690	"	1,227,138
Manufactures of iron and steel, &c.	11,824	"	5,297,116
	319,375		15,058,961

COAL USED IN THE MANUFACTURE.

Of 195,245	tons of	bar iron ham'd, &c.,	at 5	tons per ton,	976,225 tons.
Of 105,632	"	pig iron,	at 2½	"	264,080 "
Of 6,690	"	steel,	at 8	"	53,520 "
Of 11,824	"	manufactured,	at 10	"	118,824 "
Total coal imported in the form of iron,					1,412,649 "

IRON ORE USED.

For bars, ham'd iron hoops and sheets,	at 3½ tons,	650,817 tons.
For pig iron,	at 2⅔ "	281,686 "
For steel,	at 5¾ "	38,468 "
For manufactures of, &c.,	at 7 "	82,768 "
Total ore imported in the form of iron,		1,053,739 "

LIMESTONE USED.

For bars, ham'd iron hoops and sheets,	at $1\frac{1}{3}$ tons,	260,327 tons,
For pig iron,	at 1 "	105,632 "
For steel,	at $2\frac{1}{8}$ "	14,216 "
For manufactures of, &c.,	at $2\frac{2}{3}$ "	31,531 "
Total limestone imported in the form of iron,		411,706 "

BRITISH LABOUR EMPLOYED.

Three-fourths of $15,058,961	$11,294,221
Number of workmen earning say $200 per year, (which is fully 25 per cent. above the average of wages in England,) gives	56,471
Persons supported, allowing 5 per head, gives	282,355

CONSUMPTION OF BREADSTUFFS.

In Great Britain the average consumption of breadstuffs per head may be $30* per annum, which will give us the entire quantity of British breadstuffs imported in the form of iron for the last fiscal year, at	$8,470,650
The same number of people engaged in manufacturing a like quantity and description of iron in this country, would have consumed each $50 worth of the farmers' products, or	$14,117,750

which is almost identical in amount with our total exports of breadstuffs to Great Britain and Ireland for the last fiscal year.

But it is not the American agriculturists alone whose interests have been seriously prejudiced by a policy which discourages the home manufacture of iron, and permits the British manufacturer to supply us with $15,000,000 worth of iron per annum.

If we assume a locality in this country for the sake of estimating its value, where we may suppose this vast amount of iron and iron wares to be manufactured, we shall see that others who are interested in understanding the true policy of this country, have lost far more than they have gained, by depending on England for their iron.

* The average consumption of breadstuffs in the kingdom is set down by British writers at $38 per head, which would represent at that rate a total of $10,729,490.

Let us suppose this locality to have been on the Schuylkill River, near Philadelphia, than which none other could be selected more favourable to the English side of the question.

Profits to Reading and lateral roads and Schuylkill Navigation in transporting 1,412,649 tons of coal at 72 cts.,	$1,017,107
Rent to owners of coal lands on do. at 35 cts.,	494,427
Profits to coal operators on do. at 18 cts.,	254,276
Ore leave to owners of ore lands on 1,053,739 tons iron ore, at 40 cts.,	421,495
Quarry leave to owners of limestone quarries on 411,706 tons of limestone, at 10 cts.,	41,170
Interest to owners of bank stock, profits to dealers in merchandise, oil, brass, &c., &c., belonging to the head of general expenses and interest, on 319,375 tons of manufactured iron, at $4,	1,277,500
Total loss to the above interests in one year,	$3,505,975

We need say nothing further of lost benefits, in carrying the manufactured goods to market; the passenger and merchandise traffic created by such an immense business and such a large dependent population; nothing of the enhanced value it would have added to all kinds of property; nothing of increased revenue to the State, arising from increased population and new taxables, as well as that which would accrue from increased tolls on her internal improvements; nothing of the immense advantage to the whole country of keeping $15,000,000 of money at home, to be used in developing the great resources of our own country in constructing railroads and canals to cheapen and facilitate intercommunication among our own people, instead of sending that much specie every year to England, the effect of which is to derange the regular business of the country, by distri buting that great lever of trade, the currency. It would be impossible to calculate the loss which these and many other interests have sustained by discouraging the progress of the home manufacture of iron, under the delusive idea that it is the best policy to buy in the cheapest market; in which the money price, and not the labour price, is regarded as the criterion of cheapness.

From the London Mining Journal, February 2, 1850.

Average and Comparative View of Prices of Pig Iron in Glasgow, for the last twenty years.

Year	£	s.	d.	Year	£	s.	d.	Year	£	s.	d.
1830,	£5	0	0	1835,	£4	10	0	1840,	£3	15	0
1831,	4	10	0	1836,	6	15	0	1841,	3	0	0
1832,	4	10	0	1837,	4	0	0	1842,	2	10	0
1833,	4	0	0	1838,	4	0	0	1843,	2	16	0
1834,	4	5	0	1839,	4	10	0				

	1844.			1845.			1846.			1847.			1848.			1849.		
January,	£2	0	0	£3	5	0	£4	0	0	£3	13	4	£2	7	8	£2	7	0
February,	2	5	0	3	14	0	3	17	6	3	13	4	2	9	8	2	11	7
March,	2	10	0	5	5	0	3	10	0	3	11	1	2	4	6	2	9	9
April,	3	5	0	5	7	6	3	6	0	3	10	8	2	1	8	2	8	0
May,	3	5	0	4	8	0	3	10	0	3	5	3	2	4	2	2	3	9
June,	3	5	0	3	5	0	3	8	0	3	5	0	2	3	0	2	4	4
July,	3	0	0	3	5	0	3	10	0	3	8	1	2	5	3	2	5	0
August,	2	15	0	3	7	6	3	15	0	3	7	9	2	4	6	2	5	4
September,	2	10	0	4	2	0	3	13	6	3	6	0	2	4	10	2	4	0
October,	2	12	6	4	10	0	3	9	6	2	19	10	2	2	9	2	2	10
November,	2	12	6	3	17	6	3	9	0	2	11	0	2	1	9	2	4	3
December,	2	17	6	3	16	0	3	12	6	2	7	6	2	2	0	2	7	2
Average,	£2	14	0	£4	0	3	£3	11	9	£3	5	0	£2	4	4	£2	6	1

Average price for the five years, 1840 to 1844,	59s. 2d.
Ditto ditto 1845 to 1849,	61s. 5d.
Ditto ten years, 1840 to 1849,	60s. 3d.

Comparative View of Stocks on hand on 31st December.

1845,	Tons 240,000	1847,	Tons 89,000
1846,	144,300	1848,	100,000
Decrease,	95,700	Increase,	11,000
1846,	Tons 144,000	1848,	Tons 100,000
1847,	89,000	1849,	195,000
Decrease,	55,000	Increase,	95,000

Average Price of Bar Iron.

Year	£	s.	d.	Year	£	s.	d.	Year	£	s.	d.
1813,	£13	6	8	1822,	£8	1	3	1831,	£5	13	9
1814,	13	18	4	1823,	8	0	0	1832,	5	13	4
1815,	13	13	4	1824,	8	19	2	1833,	6	12	11
1816,	12	2	6	1825,	12	14	2	1834,	6	18	9
1817,	10	12	6	1826,	9	15	10	1835,	6	10	0
1818,	12	1	8	1827,	9	7	6	1836,	10	12	6
1819,	12	5	0	1828,	7	18	4	1837,	9	1	3
1820,	10	13	4	1829,	6	16	8	1838,	9	4	7
1821,	8	18	4	1830,	6	3	9	1839,	9	15	0

Average Monthly Prices of Bar Iron for the last ten years.

	1840.	1841.	1842.	1843.	1844.	1845.	1846.	1847.	1848.	1849.
January,	£9	£8	£6½	£5½	£5	£7¼	£10	£9¾	£7¾	£5¾
February,	8½	8	6½	5¼	5	8½	10	10	7¾	6
March,	8½	8	6½	5¼	5½	9¾	10	10½	7¼	6½
April,	8½	7½	6½	5¼	6	10	10	10	7¼	6½
May,	8½	7½	5½	5¼	6½	10	9½	10	7	6¼
June,	8½	7½	5½	5	6½	9	9½	10	7	6½
July,	8	7	5¼	5	6½	8½	9½	9½	6⅛	5⅞
August,	7½	7	5½	4¾	6½	8½	9½	9½	5¾	5¾
September,	8	7	6	5	6½	9	9½	9½	5¾	5⅔
October,	8½	6½	6	5	6½	10	9½	9½	5¾	5¼
November,	8½	6½	6	5	6½	10	9½	9	5¾	5⅜
December,	8½	6½	6	5	6½	10	9½	8½	5⅝	5½
Average,	£8⅜	£7¼	£5⅞	£5⅛	£6⅛	£9¼	£9⅔	£9⅔	£6⅝	£5⅞

Average—First 5 years, £6 11s. 4d.; last 5 years, £8 3s. 10d.; last 10 years, £7 7s. 6d.

Rails,	5s. to 7s. 6d. extra to prices of bars.
Sheets,	40s. ditto.
Angle Iron,	30s. ditto.
Hoops,	40s. ditto.
Best Iron,	25s. to 30s. per ton extra.

Statement, showing the total amount of revenue collected in Great Britain in 1847, *from foreign and colonial merchandize imported, and the rates of duty thereon—distinguishing the amounts received under* AD VALOREM, *from the amounts received under* SPECIFIC *duties.*

ARTICLES.	PRESENT RATE OF DUTY. FROM British Possessions.	Foreign.	NET REVENUE. Duties, ad valorem.	Duties, Specific.
	s. d.	£ *s. d.*	£	£
Arrow Root, . .	6 cwt.	2 6 cwt.		454
Cocoa, . . .	1 lb.	2 lb.		
" Husks and Shells,	½ "	1 "		21,421
Chocolate & Cocoa Paste,	2 "	6 "		
Coffee, . . .	4 "	6 "		746,436
Cotton Manufactures, wholly or in part made up, ad valorem,	5 per ct.	10 "	1,289	
Smalts, . . .		10 0 cwt.		886
*Fruits, . . from	7 6 cwt. to	1 7 6 "	2,109	568,104
Hats, ...	3 6 lb.	10 0 lb.		2,205
Isinglass, . .		5 0 cwt.		426
*Lead, . . .	5 0 ton.	1 0 0 ton.		226
*Leather Gloves, .		2 6 *a* 4 6 doz.		32,442
Linen, . . .		2½ *a* 5 sq.y.		3,900
Lawns, Sails and unenumerated articles, ad val.,		10 per ct.	931	
Liquorice, . .	10 0 cwt.	1 0 0 cwt.		11,790
Molasses, . . .		7 6 *a* 15 8 cwt.		189,814
Sperm Oil, . .		15 15 0 tun.		29,327
*Opium, . . .		1 0 lb.		2,385
Hams, ...	2 0 cwt.	7 0 cwt.		4,915
Butter, . . .	2 6 "	10 0 "		152,981
Cheese, . . .	1 6 "	5 0 "		90,207
*Eggs, . . .	2½ pr 120	10 pr 120		28,261
*Anchovies, . .		2 lb.		1,586
*Eels, . . .		13 ship load.		1,133
*Salmon, . .		10 0 cwt.		300
*Turbot and Soles, .		5 0 "		34
Rice, cleaned, . .	6 cwt.	1 0 "		2,200
" in the husk, .	1 qr.	1 0 qr.		160
Sago, . . .		6 cwt.		1,035
Caraway Seed, . .	2 6 cwt.	5 0 "		1,061
Clover " . .	do. "	5 0 "		43,835
Onion " . .	do. "	5 0 "		257
Silk manufac'd in Europe,	2 0 to £1 7*s.* 6*d.* lb			161,080
" " India, ad val.,	5 per ct.	15 per ct.	4,975	
" unenumerated, "	5 per ct.	15 per ct.	51,558	

* Articles marked thus (*) are charged 5 per cent. *of the duty* additional.

ARTICLES.	PRESENT RATE OF DUTY. FROM British Possessions.	PRESENT RATE OF DUTY. FROM Foreign.	NET REVENUE. Duties, ad valorem.	NET REVENUE. Duties, Specific.
	s. d.	£ s. d.	£	£
*Spices, . . from	1 lb. to	2 6 lb.		104,870
Rum, England, . .	8 7 gall.	}		}
" Scotland, .	4 5 "	15 0 gal.		1,316,140
" Ireland, . .	3 5 "	}		}
Brandy, and all others,		15 0 "		1,182,794
Sugar, unrefined, .	from £1 to	2 cwt.		4,372,537
" refined and Candy,	18 8 cwt.	1 11 6 "		32,300
Tallow, ...	1 "	1 6 "		77,235
*Tea, ...		2 1 lb.		5,066,494
*Tin, ...	3 0 cwt.	6 0 cwt.		931
*Tobacco, unmanufact'd,		3 0 lb.		4,165,081
" manufactured, or Cigars,		9 0 "		98,536
" Snuff, .		6 0 "		85
*Cape Wine, . .		2 9 gall.		42,332
*All other Wine, .		5 6 "		1,661,986
*Timber, ...				974,299
Woollen, manufactured, ad valorem,	5 per ct.	10 per ct.	4,393	
*Worsted Yarn, .		6 lb.		4,467
Amount collected under ad valorem duties, . .			£64,324	
Amount collected under specific duties, ...				£19,937,614
Total net revenue from Customs, ...				£20,001,938

Or not quite ⅓ of 1 per cent. of the whole is collected from ad valorem duties. Leaving out Silks, the duty received from *ad valorems* is less than £8000.

The above Table is compiled from the "Tables of the Revenue, Population, Commerce, &c., of the United Kingdom and its Dependencies, presented to both Houses of Parliament, by command of Her Majesty. Part XVII., for the year 1847." Page 16.

Of about 800 articles enumerated in the British Tariff of 1846, 400 are free, and 125 bear an ad valorem duty. A specific duty is levied upon 250, and upon 50 of these, nearly the whole of the customs revenue is collected.

It was supposed, from the course of discussions in Great Britain in reference to their tariff of 1846, that specific duties were no longer to be their chief reliance. It was to be a great step towards free trade. Yet this tariff levies nearly twenty millions sterling revenue upon fifty articles of commerce, and one-fifth of the whole upon a single article derived from this country.

The British official tables are only published to the end of the fiscal year 1847, which presents the first year's result under their tariff of 1846.

It is generally known that the tariff of the Continental countries of Europe are all based upon specific duties almost exclusively. The object is to prevent frauds upon the revenue, collusion and overtrading.

APPENDIX

TO THE

REPORT OF THE COMMITTEE ON STATISTICS, &c.

Since the adjournment of the Convention and the publication of the first report of the Committee on "Statistics and the State of the Trade," I have made a tour through the State, visiting in person, or obtaining authentic information from each of the Iron Works in the State. The facts thus collected are contained in a condensed form in the following fifteen tabular statements. The first eight of which comprise all the works in the State east of the Alleghany Mountain, and the last seven those west of that mountain. The results shown by the tables may be briefly summed up as follows:

The total number of counties in the State is - - - -	62
Of these the number now containing Iron Works is - - -	45
The number containing no Iron Works, - - - - -	17

Of these seventeen counties, however, nine contain abundance of iron ore and coal, but owing to the absence of any cheap road to market, they yet remain untouched, leaving only eight counties of sixty-two in the State not suited to the manufacture of iron.

Production of Iron from the Ore.

The following table shows the number of Furnaces of each sort and of Bloomeries in the State. The capital invested in land, buildings, and machinery. Their present capacity. The actual make in 1847, 1849, and the probable make of 1850, respectively.

		No.	Investment.	Present capacity. Tons.	Make 1847 Tons.	Make 1849. Tons.	Make 1850. Tons.
Blast furnaces using	Anthracite Coal,	57	$3,221,000	221,400	151,331	109,168	81,351
	Bituminous Coal,	7	223,000	12,600	7,800	4,900	3,900
	Coke,	4	800,000	12,000	10,000		
	Charcoal hot blast,	85	3,478,500	130,705	94,519	58,302	42,555
	" cold blast,	145	5,170,376	173,654	125,155	80,665	70,727
	Bloomeries,	6	28,700	600	545	335	280
	Totals,	304	$12,921,576	550,959	389,350	253,370	198,813

Of the 298 furnaces in the State 149, or exactly half, are in blast this year—and of this number about one-third are making no preparations to blow during next year.

The make of 1850 cannot exceed the amount above stated for this year, and will probably not equal it. It is estimated simply by deducting from the make of 1849 the amount produced by such furnaces as were at work last year and are now idle.

The estimate allows nothing for any diminution consequent on the further decline in the price of iron which has taken place since the date of my visit, nor for stoppages and failures.

Fifteen furnaces were sold by the sheriff in the first four months of this year, and other sales under execution, will probably reduce the make below the amount above stated. A comparison of the make of 1850 with that of 1847 shows a decrease of 190,537 tons, or 49 per cent. in three years. If the present state of things continues, the make of 1851 will not exceed 100,000 tons.

Conversion of Cast into Wrought Iron.

The following table shows the number of Forges and Rolling Mills in the State. The investment in lands, buildings and machinery. The total number of converting fires and their capacity per annum, and their make in 1847 and 1849.

	No. works.	Investment.	No. forge fires.	No. pud-dling fur.	Capacity. Tons.	Actual Make 1847. Tons.	Actual make 1849 Tons.
Charcoal Forges,	121	$2,026,300	402		50,250*	39,997	28,495
Rolling Mills,	79	5,554,200		436	174,400†	163,760	108,358
Totals,	200	$7,580,500	402	436	224,650	203,727	136,853

* 402 fires at 125 tons per fire per annum.
† 436 furnaces at 400 tons per furnace per annum.

The make of 1849 shows a falling off from that of 1847 of 66,874 tons, or 33 per cent.

In Eastern Pennsylvania, the manufacture of all descriptions of iron that come in competition with the English is extinct. All the markets accessible from the sea or the lakes being entirely supplied with the foreign article.

A small amount of Railroad Iron is still made for the interior, but this branch of manufacture shows the following decline:

Present annual capacity of the State,	64,400	tons Rails.
Make 1847, - - - - -	40,966	"
Make 1849, - - - - -	18,973	"

Decrease in two years 21,993 tons, or 54 per cent.

The make of 1850 will show a still greater falling off—but it cannot be accurately estimated, as the mills run or stop as they succeed or fail in obtaining contracts for their iron. Of the six Rail Mills in the State, two are stopped entirely, and the remaining four are not averaging half time.

The other Rolling Mills now running are sustained almost entirely by the manufacture of boiler plates and cut nails, which are less seriously affected by foreign competition, though the prices and the demand have been much reduced by it. The English cannot make, at any price, boiler plates equal to our best charcoal plates, but they now furnish all the inferior ones, as well as all the flue and sheet iron now sold.

Cut nails are exclusively of American invention and manufacture, and they have never been imported.*

The total number of Nail Machines in the State is 606. The annual productions of each machine averages 1000 kegs of 100 lbs. each, making 606,000 kegs, or 30,300 tons, a year. Of the product of the Forges two-thirds are sold in the form of blooms to the Rolling Mills, and are manufactured into boiler plates, horse shoe rods, and bars for the manufacture of scythes, axes, edge tools and cutlery, and other articles requiring a high polish. The remaining one-third is sold in the form of hammered bar iron in competition with Swedish and Russian iron.

*The price of Cut Nails has steadily declined in consequence of improvements in the method of manufacture and of domestic competition, from 6 cents per lb. in 1839, to 3½ cents, the present rate. It cannot be reasonably doubted that a similar result must follow the permanent establishment of other branches of the iron manufacture, and hence the fallaciousness of those arguments against initial protection, which are founded upon the assumption of a perpetual tax upon consumers.

The Conversion of Iron into Steel.

The following is a list of all the Works in the State engaged in the conversion of Steel:

	COUNTY.	SITUATION OF WORKS	OWNERS.	Amount annually conver'd Tons.
Eastern Penn'a.	Philadelphia,	Kensington,	Jas. Rowland & Co.,	600
	"	"	J. Robbins,	500
	"	"	Earp & Brink,	100
	"	"	Robt. S. Johnson,	400
	"	Oxford,	W. & H. Rowland,	700
	Lancaster,	Martic,	R. & G. D. Coleman,	400
	York,	Castlefin,	R. W. & W. Coleman,	100
West'n Pa.	Alleghany,	Pittsburg,	Singer, Hartman & Co.,	700
	"	"	Coleman, Hailman & Co.,	800
	"	"	Jones & Quigg,	1,200
	"	"	Spang & Co.,	200
	"	"	G. & J. H. Schoenberger,	200
	"	"	S. McKelvy,*	178
	Total tons,			6,078

* These works have only been in operation six months. 44 tons of the above amount is Cast Steel.

The total number of Iron Works of all kinds in the State is 504
The capital invested in lands, buildings and machinery, $20,502,076
The number of men employed, - - - - - 30,103
The number of horses employed, - - - - - - 13,562

The capital invested includes only such lands and buildings as belong to the Iron Master, and such as are directly dependant on the Iron Works for their value.

Thus the *value* of farms, grist and saw mills, and similar property, horses, wagons, tools and the like; and the dwellings of workmen near large cities, are excluded, because, though belonging to the works, they have an independent value.

The value of all coal land has been also excluded, both for the reason just given, and because it is the custom throughout the State, with very few exceptions, to purchase coal delivered at the works. The capital, and men, and horses employed in mining and transporting this coal to the works, and in transporting the finished iron to market, have also been excluded from the above account, because sufficient data were not in my possession for more than a conjectural estimate.

More than one-half of the Anthracite Furnaces, and a portion of the

Charcoal Furnaces purchase their ore of the farmers in their vicinity, who dig it on their farms and haul it to the furnaces in the winter, and at other times when they are not more particularly occupied with their agricultural labors. There are other large and valuable ore banks in the State which belong to parties who work them and sell the ore to furnaces in their vicinity. The value of all these ore banks and the number of laborers employed at them, are excluded from the above account, which comprises only such real estate as belongs to persons in the iron business, and is indispensibly requisite to carry on such business—and the *number* of men and horses directly employed by them.

The number of men thus engaged, over and above those reported to me as in the pay of the Iron Manufacturers, may be very nearly approximated by reference to tables A and B, pages 89 and 91 in the communication of S. J. Reeves, Esq., on the elementary cost of making pig and bar iron. On the basis of these tables I have calculated the number of laborers not in the pay of the Iron Masters, but directly dependant on the Iron Works for support, to be 7,081 for the Blast Furnaces, and 4,432 for the Rolling Mills, Forges, &c.; making together 11,513 to be added to the number above stated, or a grand total of 41,616 men dependant on the iron business in the State. Allowing five persons to each laborer, we have a population of 208,080 persons, or about one-tenth of the entire population of the State dependant on the manufacture of iron.

The *consumption of fuel* in all the Iron Works of the State in 1847 was as follows:

Anthracite coal, 483,000 tons, at an average value of $3 per ton, - - - - - - - - -	$1,449,000
Bituminous coal, 9,007,600 bushels, at 5, - -	450,380
Wood, - 1,490,252 cords, at $2,* - -	2,980,504
Total value, - - - - -	$4,879,884

Both wood and coal are so abundant in the State that they have scarcely any value beyond the cost of the labor of getting them to market, and the amount sent to market is only limited by the demand. So that it cannot be said that to the owner of the wood or coal, it is a

* This value is intended to include the cost of converting into Charcoal, (the form in which it is generally consumed,) and delivering at the furnace. It would be equivalent to five cents a bushel as the average value of Charcoal.

mere question as between buyers, for if the Iron Works stop, the demand and consequent production of fuel is curtailed proportionably. The wood has no value at all except for the Iron Works, as it is too bulky to bear transportation to any market; and in neighborhoods where there are no Iron Works, from $10 to $15 per acre is paid to clear and burn it off the land.

Any one not familiar with the topography of the State would suppose that the enormous consumption of one and a half million of cords of wood per annum would necessarily be of short continuance owing to a failure of the supply. But it certainly does not exceed one-fourth the ability of the State to furnish annually, for ever. The Alleghany Mountains divided into six or seven parallel ranges cross the State diagonally from north-east to to south-west. The higher portions of which ranges are too stony and steep for cultivation, but support a luxuriant growth of timber, which if cut down re-produces itself of sufficient size for the purpose of iron making, once in twenty years. Much the larger portion of these ranges has not yet been cut over the first time.

The following Statement of the Iron Works now running, or in running order, shows the number of each kind built in each period of 10 *years previous to* 1840, *and in each year since that date. Also the number of failures in each of the last* 10 *years.*

		Blast Furnaces.				Bloomeries, forges and rolling mills.		Total of all kinds.	
		Mineral coal		Charcoal.					
		Built.	S F*	Built.	S F*	Built	S F*	Built.	S F*
10 years ending January 1st,	1730					1		1	
	1740			1		1		2	
	1750			2		1		3	
	1760			2		5		7	
	1770								
	1780			3		2		5	
	1790			1		4		5	
	1800			9		16		25	
	1810			11		19		30	
	1820			14		16		30	
	1830	1		18		30		49	
10 years ending January 1st,	1840	5		72		46		123	
During the year	1840	3		3	3	6	3	12	6
	1841	1		3	1	2	1	6	2
	1842	5	2	8	8	7	10	20	20
	1843		1	5	4	2	2	7	7
	1844	4	6	13	2	4	3	21	11
	1845	14		15	2	11	1	40	3
	1846	11	1	30	3	12		53	4
	1847	8	1	12	15	5	8	25	24
	1848	5	5	6	20	6	12	17	37
	1849	3	5	2	30	5	6	10	41
4 months in	1850	3			15	4	7	7	22
Now unfinished,		5				1		6	
Totals,		68	21	230	103	206	53	504	177

* Sold by Sheriff or failed since January, 1840.

That portion of the preceding table which relates to the period prior to 1840 is of historical interest only. It shows a very regular increase in the number of works. The course of affairs for the last ten years is very clearly indicated by the table.

The great impetus given to the business about the year 1840, may be attributed to the discovery two years before, of the value of anthracite coal for iron making purposes. The lower clauses of the compromise tariff act coming into operation in 1842, and the passage of a new tariff act in that year together, produce the curious result of 20 new works built and 20 failures. The number of new works then steadily increases, and the number of failures as steadily decreases, until they stand in 1846—fifty-three new works built to four failures. But in that year the tariff of 1842 was repealed, and the present ad valorem duty laid on the price of foreign iron, which was then excessively inflated by the railway fever in England, and in the next year, (1846,) we have the number of new works and the number of failures again even, (25 to 24,) as in 1842, but with this important difference, that in 1842 distress was decreasing, whereas the difficulties of 1847 were only the beginning of more serious troubles. This is shown by the regularly diminishing number of new works, and the as regularly increasing number of failures, until we have for 1849 the new works only ten to forty-one failures.

The result has been asserted to be entirely the effect of over-trading, and to be in no respect attributable to the tariff of 1846—but it will be seen by reference to the extract from Mr. Walker's report, on page 36, that at the very time when we were making most iron, we were importing annually an average of 50,000 tons of pig and bar iron alone, exclusive of all chains, wrought iron, hardware, cutlery and steel, &c., &c. A business cannot be said to be overdone which is inadequate to the supply of the home market.

It may be well to note one other fact shown by the preceding statement. The year 1847 was that in which the largest amount of iron was produced, and also the first of the present series of disastrous years.

It is the custom with the manufacturers of Charcoal Iron to make their contracts in the winter for all the materials required during the year. The prices of these materials is governed by the selling price of iron at that time, but the greater part of a year elapses before the iron is made and brought to market.

By reference to page 37 it will be seen that the price of Scotch pig in Glasgow in January, 1847, was - - - - -	£3 13 4	
January, 1848, it was - - - - - -	2 8 4	
Decrease in price, - - - -		£1 5 0
Freights in January, 1847, were - -	12s. 6d.	
" " 1848, " - - -	15s. 0d.	
Difference, - - - - -		2 6
		£1 2 6
Add decrease in duty 30 per cent. *ad valorem*, - -		7 6
Total decrease in price of iron in the United States,		£1 10 0
Or in dollars, - - - - - - - - -		$7 33

Makers of small capital having contracted for their materials at the high prices ruling in the beginning of the year, and being obliged to sell at the low ones prevailing toward the close of it, were reduced to bankruptcy.

It will be seen by reference to the statement that two-thirds of the failures in the year were among the makers of Charcoal Pig Iron.

Many other interesting deductions might be made from the tables, but the object of this brief introduction is only to point out a few of the more striking results. Leaving to abler hands their more careful analysis, they are respectfully submitted.

CHARLES E. SMITH,
Chairman Committee on Statistics.

EXPLANATIONS

REFERRING TO THE FOLLOWING TABLES.

The *ton of iron* is always the gross ton of - - 2,240 lbs.
Except *Blooms and Puddled Bar*, which are bought and sold
by the Ankoney or double gross ton of - - - 2,464 lbs.
And Nails, which are sold by the net ton of - - 2,000 lbs.
Anthracite Coal is sold by the gross ton - - - 2,240 lbs.
Bituminous Coal by the bushel of - - - - - 80 lbs.

In the statement of the Blast Furnaces in the column headed "kind of ore used,"

H signifies Brown Hematite ore.
M " Magnetic ore.
F " Fossiliferous Red Oxyd or Fossil ore.
C " Argillaceous Carbonate.
B " Bog ore.

In the column headed "Blast—Tuyeres—Diam.," the figures represent the diameter of the blowing nozzles.

In the column headed "Pressure," the figures represent the pressure to the square inch in pounds avoirdupoise.

In the column headed "Market"
"E" means Philadelphia.
"W" " Pittsburg.
"H" " Home—or the vicinity of the works.

In the column headed "kind of metal made"
1 signifies coarse grey or best foundry iron.
2 " close grey iron.
3 " mottled and white iron or hard iron.

In some instances there are figures in the column headed "Situation, Post Office," where such occur they signify the distance of the works from the Post Office.

The Hot Blast Furnaces which have dates assigned them prior to 1830, were built for Cold Blast Furnaces, and have been since changed to Hot Blast.

TABLE OF CONTENTS.

*

The Tables succeed in the following order.

EASTERN PENNSYLVANIA.

A Detailed Statement of the Forges in Eastern Pennsylvania, in the year 1850, not properly belonging to either of the other classes.

A Detailed Statement of the Charcoal Forges in Eastern Pennsylvania, in the year 1850.

A Detailed Statement of all the Rolling Mills in Eastern Pennsylvania, in the year 1850.

WESTERN PENNSYLVANIA.

Statement, showing the number and condition of each sort of Iron Works, and the capital invested in the Land and Buildings in each County in Western Pennsylvania, in the year 1850.

A Detailed Statement of all the Charcoal Hot Blast Furnaces in Western Pennsylvania, in the year 1850.

A Detailed Statement of all the Raw Bituminous Coal Hot Blast Furnaces in Pennsylvania, in the year 1850.

A Detailed Statement of all the Coke Hot Blast Furnaces in the State of Pennsylvania, in the year 1850.

A Detailed Statement of all the Charcoal Cold Blast Furnaces in Western Pennsylvania, in the year 1850.

A Detailed Statement of all the Charcoal Forges in Western Pennsylvania, in the year 1850.

A Detailed Statement of all the Rolling Mills in Western Pennsylvania, in the year 1850.

A Detailed Statement of all the CHARCOAL FORGES IN WESTERN PENNSYLVANIA in the year 1850.

COUNTY.	Date of Sheriff's sale or failure.	Kind of power employed.	Date of construction.	NAME OF WORKS.	SITUATION. P. O.	OWNERS.	No. forge fires	No. hammers.	Largest Product.	Actual make 1849		Men and boys employed.	Horses, mules and oxen employed.	Market.	No. run out. Fires.
									Tons.	Bars.	Blooms.				
Clarion,		Water,	1833	Shippenville,	Shippenville,	Shippen & Black,	2	1	150	50		16	4	Home,	1
Indiana,	1845 S	"	1841	Indiana,	Armagh,	Elias Baker,	2	1	200	20	100	18	6	"	1
Somerset,	1850 S	"	1826	Shade,	Stoystown,	Shryock, Bingham & Co.,	1	1	30	30		8	3	"	
	2		3				5	3	380	100	100	42	13		2

A Detailed Statement of all the RAW BITUMINOUS COAL HOT-BLAST FURNACES IN PENNSYLVANIA, in the year 1850.

COUNTY.	Date of Sheriff's sale or failure.	No. Furnaces. In Blast.	No. Furnaces. Out of Blast.	Date of construction.	NAME OF WORKS.	SITUATION. P. O.	OWNERS.	LESSEES.	Kind of ore used.	Largest Product. Tons.	Actual make 1849, Tons.	No. Men and boys employed.	No. oxen, Horses, and mules employed.	BLAST. Tuyeres. No.	BLAST. Tuyeres. Diam.	BLAST. Pressure.	STACK. Bosh. feet.	STACK. Height. feet.	Kind of Power used.	Kind of metal made and No.	Capacity.
Mercer,			1	1845	Middlesex,	Middlesex,	Sennett, Lester & Co.,	None.	C.	1,400	1,000	80	30	2	3		10	37	Steam.	1, 2	2,000
"		1		1846	Sharon,	Sharon,	Schoenburger, Agnew & Co.,	"	C.	1,750	1,750	80	20	3	3		10	40	Steam.	2, 3	2,000
"		1		1845	Clay,	Clarksville,	Himrod, Vincent & Co.,	"	C.	1,150	1,150	75	30	2	3	2	8½	37	"	2, 3	1,600
"		1		1845	Shenango,	Mercer,	McFarland & King,	"	C.	1,000	1,000	60	25	2	3	2	8	36	W. & S.	2, 3	1,500
"	1848 F		1	1846	Harriet,	Greenville,	Dr. Wm. Irvin,	"	C.	800		80	40	2	3		10	55	Steam.	3	2,000
"	1848 F		1	1846	Mary Ann,	do.	do.	Whitaker & Watson.	C.	1,200		80	50	3	3		10	50	"	3	2,000
"	1848 F		1	1847	Blanche,	Sharon,	McClure & Co.,	None.	C.	500		60	25	3	3		8	40	"	3	1,500
	3	3	4							7,800	4,900	515	220								

A Detailed Statement of all the COKE HOT-BLAST FURNACES IN THE STATE OF PENNSYLVANIA in the year 1850.

COUNTY.	Sold by Sheriff, or failed.	No. Furnaces. In Blast.	No. Furnaces. Out of Blast.	Date of construction.	NAME OF WORKS.	SITUATION. P. O.	OWNERS.	Ore.	Bushels Coal consumed.	Largest Product. Tons.	Actual make 1849. Tons.	No. Men and boys employed.	No. oxen, Horses, mules employed.	BLAST. Tuyeres. No.	BLAST. Tuyeres. Diam.	STACK. Bosh. feet.	STACK. Height. feet.	Kind of Power used and No.	Kind of metal made and No.	Capacity.
Armstrong,	1844 S		1	1840	Brady's Bend,	Brady's Bend,	M. P. Sawyer and others, of Boston,	C.						3	2½a3	11	40	Steam.	2, 3	2,000
"	1844 S		1	1841	"	"	"	"	1,120,000	10,000	0	900	100	3	"	11	40	"	"	2,000
"	1844 S		1	1843	"	"	"	"						3	"	13	50	"	"	3,500
"	1844 S		1	1846	"	"	"	"							"	14	50	"	"	4,500
	4		4																	12,000

A Detailed Statement of all the ROLLING MILLS IN WESTERN PENNSYLVANIA in the year 1850.

COUNTY.	Date of Sheriff's sale or failure.	Date of construction.	NAME OF WORKS.	SITUATION. POST OFFICE.	OWNERS.	Number puddling fur.	Number heating fur.	Number Trains. Rolls.	No. Nail Machines.	CONSUMED. Bituminous Coal. Bushels.	CONSUMED. Wood. Cords.	CONSUMED. Pig. Tons.	CONSUMED. Bloom. Tons.	CONSUMED. Scrap. Tons.	Largest Product. Tons.	No. furnaces running, 1850. Puddling	No. furnaces running, 1850. Heating.	Men and boys employed.	Horses, mules and oxen employed.	No. and kind of power employed.	Actual make 1849. Tons.	No. run out Fires.	No. Forge fires.	Description of Iron made.	Remarks.
Alleghany,		1836	Pittsburg,	Pittsburg,	Lorentz, Sterling & Co.,	14	6	5	25	480,000	500	6,000	500	500	5,500	14	6	250	10	Steam,	5,500	1	1	Bar, Rod, Hoop, Sheet, Boiler, Nails, Spikes.	
"		1824	Kensington,	"	Carothers, Miller & Co.,	11	5	5	14	360,000		5,000	500	200	4,500	11	5	160	10	"	4,500	1			
"		1835	Wayne,	"	Bailey, Brown & Co.,	11	6	4	16	300,000		4,500	300	100	4,000	11	6	150	10	"	2,500	1			
"		1845	Lippincott,	"	Graff, Lindsay & Co.,	9	7	4	14	300,000		4,700	250	150	4,000	9	7	150	4	"	4,000	1			
"		1825	Sligo,	"	Lyon, Shorb & Co.,	6	9	4	13	320,000		2,650	3,870	300	5,432	6	7	156	3	"	4,241	1			Enlarged 1837.
"		1823	Juniata,	"	G. & J. H. Schoenberger,	14	12	5	50	410,000		5,000	1,000	1,000	5,500	14	10	295	18	"	4,900	1			" 1845.
"		1828	Ætna,	"	Spang & Co.,	11	8	4	25	300,000		4,500	500	200	4,100	10	5	150	24	"	3,000	1			" 1838.
"		1840	Hecla,	"	Wood & McKnight,	11	5	3	15	300,000		5,000	100		4,000	11	5	150	26	"	3,500	1			
"		1849	Eagle,	"	Jas. Wood & Co.,	10	5	4	31	200,000		2,800			2,100	10	5	108	4	"	2,100	1			
"		1846	Clinton,	"	Cuddy, Jones & Co.,	10	6	4	11	177,300		2,566	60		2,900	10	6	102	6	"	2,029	1			
"		1828	Juniata,	Alleghany City,	Semple, Bissell & Co.,	9	4	4	13	300,000		4,000	500	300	3,700	8	4	125	6	"	3,000	1			
"		1845	Vesuvius,	Pittsburg,	Lewis, Dalzell & Co.,	9	6	4	19	260,000		3,000	50	50	2,250	8	5	120	8	"	2,000	1			
"		1849	Pennsylvania,	"	Everson, Preston & Co.,	2	3	2		75,000	400	50	50	100	150	2	3	35	4	"	150		1	Rods, Shafts, Anchors, Axles.	Running half time.
"		1849	Sheffield,	"	Singer, Hartman & Co.,	2	6	2		150,000		600	1,200	200	1,800	2	6	80	3	"	1,800			"	
"		1844	Duquesne,	"	Coleman, Hailman & Co.,		4	4		120,000			1,000	1,200	1,800		4	80	4	"	1,800			Boiler & Sheet Iron & Sheet Steel.	
"		1845	Pittsburg Steel,	"	Jones & Quigg,		3	1		100,000			900	450	1,200		2	50	2	"	1,200			Bar and Sheet Steel and Iron.	
Armstrong,	1844 S	1841	Brady's Bend,	Brady's Bend,	M. P. Sawyer and others,	26	10	2		672,000		9,000			7,200	20	4	200	20	"		1		Rails.	
"		1848	Kittanning,	Kittanning,	Brown, Phillips & Co.,	10	5	4	12	360,000		3,300			2,500	8	5	150	5	"	2,500	1		Bar, Rod, Sheet, Plate, Hoops and Nails.	Running half time.
Fayette,		1834	Fairchance,	Uniontown,	F. H. Oliphant & Son,	2	3	3	6	100,000		900		40	700	2	3	60	12	"	700	1	1		
"	1847 S	1842	Brownsville,	Brownsville,	E. Hughes, lessee,	4	4	3	10	150,000		2,000	50	50	1,500	4	3	75	10	"	600	1	2		
Lawrence,		1842	Cossallo,	New Castle,	Cossallo Iron Co.,	8	4	3	25	150,000		3,000		200	2,500	8	4	130	200	"	1,700	2			Running half time.
"		1847	Orizaba,	"	Peebles & Co.,	4	4	3	21	160,000		3,200		100	2,600	8	4	130	200	"	1,000	1			
Venango,		1844	Franklin,	Franklin,	H. Coulter & Co.,	4	3	3	10	120,000		1,500		60	1,200	4	3	104	12	Water,	900				
Total No. Mills,	2	23				187	128	80	330	5,864,300	900	73,266	10,830	5,200	72,132	180	112	3,010	601		53,620	19	5		

A Detailed Statement of all the CHARCOAL HOT-BLAST FURNACES IN WESTERN PENNSYLVANIA in the year 1850.

COUNTY.	Date of Sheriff's sale or failure.	No. furnaces. In.	No. furnaces. Out.	Date of construction	NAME OF WORKS.	SITUATION. POST OFFICE.	OWNERS.	Kind of ore used.	Largest Product. Tons.	Actual make 1849. Tons.	No. men and boys employed.	No. horses and mules employed	No. tuyeres	Diam. Bosh. feet.	Height feet.	Kind of Power used.	Kind metal and No.	Capacity. Tons.	Remarks.
Armstrong, 1	1844 S	1		1339	Buffalo,	Worthington,	P. Graff & Co.,	C.	1,800	1,800	80	50	2	9	32	W.&S.	3	1,800	
Cambria, 2		1		1346	Ben's Creek,	Johnstown,	G. S. King & Co.,	H.	1,080	1,080	90	35	2	9	30	Water,	2, 3	1,800	
"	1848 S		1	1346	Eliza,	Ebensburg,	Ritter & Irvin,	H.	1,000		90	45	2	9	30	"	3	1,800	
Clarion, 1	1842 S	1		1333	Lucinda,	Lucinda,	Reynolds & Buchanan,	C.	1,429	1,280	80	45	1	7, 10	30	"	1, 2	1,450	Leased by Reynolds & Evans.
Indiana, 2	1845 S	1		1842	Indiana,	Armagh,	Elias Baker,	H.	1,100	900	80	36	2	9	30	"	2, 3	1,800	Bosh 7 feet until 1847.
"		1		1846	Blacklick,	"	Schoenberger, King & Co.,	"	1,000	756	80	46	1	8	30	"	2, 3	1,400	
Lawrence, 1		1		1848	Wilmington,	Wilmington,	Cassallo Iron Co.,	C.	1,400	1,400	100	50	3	10	34	Steam,	2, 3	2,000	
Mercer, 6	1848 F		1	1846	Hamburg,	Delaware Grove,	John Warden,	"	800	800	75	30	2	10	38	"	1, 2	2,000	
"	1848 F		1	1848	Harry of the West,	Georgetown,	Dr. Wm. Irvin,	"	500	500	80	50	3	9	40	"	2, 3	1,800	Leased by Whitaker & Watson.
"		1		1846	Mineral Ridge,	"	Ward & Co.,	"	900	400	75	33	2	8, 6	34	"	2, 3	1,600	
"			1	1846	Sandy No. 2,	Pryon,	Gen. C. M. Read,	"	600		50	30	2	8		Water,	3	1,400	
"			1	1838	" " 1,	"	"	"	500		50	30	2	7		"	3	1,000	
"	1849 S		1	1846	Mazeppa,	Mercer,	J. P. Garrett & Co.,	"	800		60	35	2	7, 6	33	Steam,	2, 3	1,000	
Somerset, 1	1850 S		1	1812	Shade,	Stoystown,	Shryock, Bingham & Co.,	C. H.	900	750	80	43	1	8	30	Water,	2, 3	1,400	Abandoned 1828, rebuilt 1846.
Venango, 2	1847 S		1	1845	Orleans,	Franklin,	Reymond & Grey,	C.	700	700	50	45	3	9	27, 6	"	2, 3	1,800	
"		1		1832	Rockland,	Rockland,	Dempsey & Wick,	"	550	200	50	40	1	8, 6	28	Steam,	2	1,600	Leased by J. Dempsey.
Westmoreland, 2		1		1847	Conemaugh,	Armagh,	McGill & Foster,	H.	800	600	60	30	2	9	33	"	3	1,800	
"	1848 S	1		1846	Laurel Hill,	West Fairfield,	Hoover & McCallister,	"	800	800	80	40	2	9	33	Water,	3	1,800	
	10	10	8						16,659	11,966	1,310	713						29,230	

Total number furnaces 18

STATEMENT, showing the number and condition of each sort of IRON WORKS, and the capital invested in the Land and Buildings in each County in WESTERN PENNSYLVANIA, in the year 1850.

FURNACES.

COUNTY.	RAW BITUMINOUS COAL AND HOT BLAST					COKE AND HOT BLAST.					CHARCOAL AND HOT BLAST.					CHARCOAL AND COLD BLAST.					FORGES.			ROLLING MILLS.			TOTAL.			Counties.
	S.* F.	In.	Out.	Total.	Investment.	S.* F.	In.	Out.	Total.	Investment.	S.* F.	In.	Out.	Total.	Investment.	S.* F.	In.	Out.	Total.	Investment.	S.* F.	Total No.	Investment.	S.* F.	Total No.	Investment.	S.* F.	Total No.	Investment.	
1. Allegheny,																									16	1,837,000		16	1,837,000	1.
2. Armstrong,						4	0	4	4	800,000	1	1		1	38,000	5	7	4	11	374,560				1	2	175,000	11	18	1,387,560	2.
3. Beaver,																														3.
4. Butler,																1	4	2	6	190,000							1	6	190,000	4.
5. Cambria,											1	1	1	2	77,000		3	1	4	145,000							1	6	222,000	5.
6. Clarion,											1	1		1	40,000	6	22	6	28	1,177,166		1	4,000				7	30	1,221,166	6.
7. Crawford,																														7.
8. Elk,																														8.
9. Erie,																		1	1	12,000								1	12,000	9.
10. Fayette,																4	3	2	5	151,500				1	2	115,000	5	7	266,500	10.
11. Forest,																														11.
12. Greene,																														12.
13. Indiana,											1	2		2	85,000	2		2	2	48,000	1	1	5,000				4	5	138,000	13.
14. Jefferson,																														14.
15. Lawrence,												1		1	40,000			1	1	20,000					2	250,000		4	310,000	15.
16. McKean,																														16.
17. Mercer,	3	3	4	7	223,000						3	1	5	6	180,000	1		3	3	68,000							7	16	471,000	17.
18. Somerset,											1		1	1	20,000	2		2	2	35,000	1	1	5,000				4	4	60,000	18.
19. Venango,											1	1	1	2	40,000	11	8	10	18	487,650					1	48,500	12	21	576,150	19.
20. Warren,																														20.
21. Washington,																														21.
22. Westmoreland,											1	2		2	91,000	2	2	2	4	105,000							3	6	196,000	22.
	3	3	4	7	223,000	4	0	4	4	800,000	10	10	8	18	611,000	34	49	36	85	2,813,876	2	3	14,000	2	23	2,425,500	55	140	6,887,376	

22 Counties—13 Counties having Iron Works.

* Sold by Sheriff or failed since 1840.

A Detailed Statement of all the BLOOMERY FORGES IN EASTERN PENNSYLVANIA, in the year 1850.

COUNTY.	Sold by Sheriff, or failed.	Date of construction.	NAME OF WORKS.	SITUATION. P. O.		OWNERS.	LESSEES.	Kind of Power employed.	No. Bloom'y fires.	No. Hammers.	Largest Product. Tons.	Actual make 1849.	Form in which Iron leaves the Works.	Men and boys employed.	Horses, mules and oxen employed.	MARKET.
Carbon,		1830	Maria,	Lehighton,		T. M. Smith and Est. of Richards,	None.	Water.	2	1	10	10	Bars.	6	2	Home.
"		1848	Pine Run,	do.	5	J. & D. Lowrey,	"	"	1	1	65	65	"	25	12	"
"		1820	Ashland,	Lehigh Gap,	7	J. J. Albright,	"	"	2	1	80	80	"	12	8	"
"		1843	Anthony's,	do.	7½	N. Anthony,	"	"	2	1	40	40	"	12	4	"
Monroe,		1829	Analomink,	Stroudsburg,		John Jordan, Jr.,	Jas. Bell, Jr.	"	3	2	280	100	"	30	12	"
Northampton,	1847 F	1805	Jacobsburg,	Jacobsburg,		A. Benade,	C. E. Benade.	"	2	1	70	40	"	12	2	"
									12	7	545	335		97	40	

These six works all use the rich Magnetic Ores from New Jersey, and consume about 3 tons of ore and 15 cords of wood to the ton of bars produced. The average annual capacity is 50 tons per fire, which, for the 12 fires in the State, would give 600 tons of bars, consuming 9000 cords of wood, and 1800 tons of ore.

A Detailed Statement of the FORGES IN EASTERN PENNSYLVANIA, in the year 1850, not properly belonging to either of the other classes.

COUNTY.	Sold by Sheriff, or failed.	Date of construction.	NAME OF WORKS.	SITUATION. P. O.	OWNERS.	No. Pudding Fur.	No. Heating Fur.	No. forge fires.	CONSUMED. Bitum's Coal. Tons.	Anthra'e Coal. Tons.	Wood. Cords.	Pig. Tons.	Bloom. Tons.	Scrap. Tons.	Largest Product. Tons.	No Furnaces running, 1850. Pudding	No Furnaces running, 1850. Heating.	Men and boys employed.	Horses, mules and oxen employed.	Description of Iron made.	Kind of Power employ'd	Actual make 1849.	Capacity.
Berks,	1848 S	1846	Reading,	Reading,	A. Taylor,		2			1000			450		400			14	3	Axles.	Steam.		600
Cumberland,	1849 S	1848	Holley,	Papertown,	F. & M. Bank, Philada.,	2	1			800		1000			10			25	6	Blooms.	"		800
Philadelphia,		1849	Kensington,	Kensington,	J. Rowland & Co.		1		600				500	100			1	7	1	Steel plates.	"		1000
"		1850	Oxford,	Frankford,	W. & H. Rowland,			3			1500			1000				13	2	Saw plates.	"		600
						2	4	3	600	1800	1500	1000	950	1100	410		1	59	12				3000

A Detailed Statement of all the COLD BLAST CHARCOAL FURNACES IN EASTERN PENNSYLVANIA, in the year 1850.

COUNTY.	Sold by Sheriff, or failed.	No Furnaces. In Blast	No Furnaces. Out Blast.	Date of construction.	NAME OF WORKS.	SITUATION. POST OFFICE.	OWNERS.	LESSEES.	Kind of Ores used.	Largest Product (Tons.)	Actual make in 1849. (Tons.)	No. of men and boys employed	No. oxen, horses and mules employed.	BLAST. Cold.	BLAST. Tuyeres No.	BLAST. Tuyeres Diam.	BLAST. Pressure.	STACK. Bosh feet.	STACK. Height. feet.	Kind of Power used.	Kind of Metal made.	Market for sales.	Capacity (Tons.)
Adams,			1	1830	Chesnut Grove,	Whitestown,	J. V. Boggs,	None.	M.	500		56	35	cold.	1			8	32	Water.			1,100
Blair,		1		1824	Bald Eagle,	Warrior's Mark, Huntingd'n Co.	Lyon, Shorb & Co.		H.	1,830	1,700	118	40	"	1	2½		8½	34	"	3	W.	1,830
do.		1		1819	Rebecca,	Martinsburg,	D. P. Schoenberger,		H.	1,500	1,300	60	50	"	1	"		8½	32	"	3	W.	1,500
do.		1		1846	Bloomfield,	Sarah,	"		H.	1,350	1,000	75	32	"	1	"		8½	30	Steam.	3	W.	1,350
do.		1		1833	Sarah,	"	"		H.	1,400	1,200	70	55	"	1	"		8½	32	Water.	3	W.	1,400
Bedford,	1848 S		1	1841	Lemnos,	Hopewell,	Thos. King & Co.		¼ F. & H.	400	291	74	30	"	1	2½		8½	30	Steam.	3	H. & W.	1,350
Berks,		1		1759	Hopewell,	Douglasville,	Clement, Brooke & Co.		M.	1,150	1,000	80	50	"	1		¾	6½	30	Water.	1	E.	1,150
do.		1		1816	Mossilm,	Mossilm,	N. V. R. Hunter,	F. S. Hunter.	H.	1,200	1,200	60	54	"	1	2		8.9	32	"	2, 3	"	1,350
do.		1		1793	Joanna,	Joanna,	Darling & Smith,		M.	1,050	1,050	50	30	"	1			7.6	31	"	2, 3	"	1,050
do.		1		1827	Mount Penn,	Reading, 4 m.	John Schwartz,		M.	1,050	897	100	64	"	1	2⅛		8	31	"	2, 3	"	1,100
do.		1		1797	Mary Ann,	Long Swamp,	Hort. Trexler,		M. & H.	1,000	800	59	35	"	1	2⅛		7	30	"	1, 3	"	1,000
do.		1		1791	Sally Ann,	New Jerusalem,	J. V. R. Hunter,		H.	850	750	60	40	"	1	2⅛		6	32	"	1, 2, 3	"	850
do.			1	1835	Oley,	Oley,	Jacob S. Spang,		M. & H.	800		60	35	"	1		¾	6½	28	"	1	"	800
do.	1842 S		1	before 1770	Old Oley,	Pricetown,	George Merkel,		M. & H.	800				"	1			9	28	"	1	"	1,400
Cumberland,	1846 S		1	1826	Mary Ann,	Shippensburg,	Carlisle Bank,		H.	800		80	25	"	1	2½		8	32	"	3	"	1,100
do.	1846 S		1	1828	Augusta,	"	J. M. Haldeman,		H.	800		80	25	"	1	2½		8	32	S.&W.	3	"	1,100
do.	1847 S		1	1815	Carlisle,	Carlisle,	Peter F. Ege,		H.	875		56	29	"	1	1¾		7½	25	Water.	2	"	1,000
do.	1849 F		1	1794	Cumberland,	Dickinson,	Thomas C. Miller,		⅓ M. & H.	400	247	40	25	"	1	2		8½	30	"	2, 3	"	1,350
do.	1847 S		1	1836	Big Pond,	Shippensburg,	Schoch, Sons & Co.		F. & H.	871	871	75	50	"	1	2½		7½	30	"	3	"	1,000
Columbia,	1847 S	1		1815	Catawissa,	Maineville,	B. P. Frick,		F.	750	500	53	50	"	1	3½		8½	32	"	1, 2	"	1,350
Centre,	1843 S		1	1832	Martha,	Martha Furnace P. O.	Rowland Curtin & Sons,		H.	1,180		70	60	"	1	2½		8	32	"	3	"	1,180
do.	1843 S	1		1848	Eagle,	Milesburg,	C. & J. Curtin,		H.	800	800	80	45	"	2	2¼		8	30	"	3	"	1,100
do.		1		1800	Logan,	Bellefonte,	Valentines & Thomas,		H.	1,320	1,320	40	36	"	1	3	⅜	8	31	"	3	"	1,320
do.	1850 F	1		1816	Rock,	Bellefonte, 5 m.	Samuel Edmiston,		H.	700	700	35	36	"	1	1¾		7	28	"	3	"	900
do.	1844 S		1	1828	Hannah,	Centre Line,	Lyon, Shorb & Co.	Campbell, Stevens & Co.	H.	1,261	800	100	40	"	1	2½		8½	33	"	3	W.	1,350
do.	1849 S		1	1835	Juliana,	Juliana,	John Adams,		H.	1,000	250	60	30	"	1	2½		8½	33	"	3	E.	1,350
do.		1	1	1830	Howard,	Howard,	Irvin, Thomas & Co.		⅛ F. & H.	1,400	1,400	50	30	"	1	"		8½	33	"	3	"	1,400
Clinton,	1839 S		1	1834	Sugar Valley,	Loganville,	J. T. Hale,		H.	400				"	1						1	"	800
do.	1839 S		1	1831	Lamar,	Salona,	Solomon McCormick,		H.	750				"	1			8		"	2, 3	"	1,100
Chester,		1		1835	Isabella,	Rockville,	David Potts & Co.		M.	1,000	1,000	75	45	"	1	2¼		6½	33	"	2, 3	"	1,000
do.		1		1736	Warwick,	Pottstown,	David Potts, Jr.		M.	1,400	1,100	100	50	"	1	2¼		7	33	"	2, 3	"	1,400
Dauphin,	1847 S	1		1849	Middletown,	Middletown,	Peters & Gamber,	Grubb & Cabean.	M.		470	70	42	"	1	2		6½	30	"	1	"	800
do.	1847 S	1		1833	"	"	"	"	M.					"	1	2		8½	"	"	1	"	1,350
Franklin,	1849 S	1		1800	Carrick,	Faussetsburg, 4 m.	N. Kelley,	Witherow & Walker.	H.	400		10	5	"	1	2½		7½	30	"	2, 3	H.	1,000
do.	1849 S		1	1830	Southampton,	Shippensburg, 3½,	Alfred Bujac,		H.	900		60	33	"	1	2		9½	30	"	1, 2, 3	E.	1,500
do.	1849 S		1	1835	Mary,	" 4,	"		H.	1,100	360	60	33	"	1	2		9	30	"	1, 2, 3	"	1,400
do.			1	1828	Franklin,	St. Thomas, 4,	B. Phreaner & Sons,		H.	800	110			"	1	1½		9	30	"	2, 3	H.	1,400
do.			1	1825	Valley,	Louden, 2,	John Beaver,	Scheffler & Son.	H.	300	50	15	6	"	1	1½		6	28	"	2, 3	H.	800
do.			1	1835	Warren,	Sylvan,	Bowers' heirs,		H.	227		35	6	"	1	1¼		8	28	"	2	E.	1,100
Huntingdon,	1849 S		1	1846	Rebecca,	McElavey Fort P. O.	A. G. Curtin,		F.	700	700	40	23	"	1	1¾		6½	27	"	3	"	800
do.		1		1813	Pennsylvania,	Baileysville,	Lyon, Shorb & Co.		H.	2,309	1,792	120	50	"	1	2½		8½	35	"	3	W.	2,310
do.	1847 S	1		1833	Greenwood,	14 miles from Lewistown,	John A. Wright & Co.		H.	1,069	729	100	67	"	1	2½ 3		8½	32.4	"	2, 3	E.	1,200
do.	1848 S		1	1846	Malinda,	Orbisonia,	Blair & Madden,		H.	350		30	20	"	1	2½		6½	28	"	2, 3	"	800
do.		1		1829	Paradise,	Paradise Furnace,	H. Trexler & Co.		¾ F. & ¼ H.	700	560	35	24	"	2	2		7½	33	"	2, 3	"	1,000
do.	1849 S		1	1838	Jackson,	McElavey Fort,	Mitchell, Vance & Alexander,		F.	350		30	18	"	1	2		6	20	"	3	"	800
Lehigh,	1850 S		1	1800	Hampton,	Lionsville,	Seyfert, McManus & Co.		H.	650		46	26	"	1	2		9	32	"	2, 3	"	800
Lycoming,		1		1838	Heshbon,	Newberry,	Wm. McKinney,		H.	550	400	30	30	"	1	2		6.9	25	"	3	E. & H.	900
do.			1	1820	Pine Creek,	Jersey Shore, 4 m.	J. Vickers,		F.	1,000		60	36	"	1	2		8	30	"	1, 2	H.	1,100
Lancaster,		1		1785	Mount Hope,	Mount Hope,	E. & B. Grubb,		M.	1,434	1,434	57	48	"	1	2		6½	27	"	1, 2	E.	1,434
do.			1	1846	Lancaster,	Lancaster,	George Ford,		H.	500	300	16	4	"	2	2½		7½	33	Steam.	2, 3	"	1,000
Lebanon,		1		1745	Cornwall,	Cornwall,	R. W. Coleman,		M.	1,405	750	60	46	"	1	2		7½	30	S.&W.	1	"	1,400
do.		1		1745	Colebrooke,	Elizabethtown, Lancaster Co.	Wm. Coleman,		M.	1,600	1,400	60	60	"	1	2		9	30	Water.	1	"	1,600
do.			1	1837	Monroe,	Fredericksburg,	Jonathan Seidel,	Seidel & Thompson.	M.	500		40	25	"	1	2		7	30	"	1	"	900
Mifflin,			1	1830	Marion,	Perryville,	W. & T. Reed,		H.	1,800		80	35	"	1					"	2, 3	"	1,800
Montgomery,			1	1836	Green Lane,	Sumneytown,	Wm. Schall,		H.	450		50	18	"	1	2⅛		7.4	33	"	2, 3	"	900
Northumberland,	1848 S		1	1847	Paxinas,	Paxinas,	Taggert & Co.		*F.	300	300	35	12	"	2	2¼		8	30	"	3	"	1,100
Perry,	1841 S		1	1833	Caroline,	Bailysburg,	James Bailey,		F.	750	166	40	10	"	1	2½		9	25	Steam.	3	"	1,400
do.			1	1830	Oak Grove,	Landisburg,	Thudium & Co.		F. & H.	800		50	12	"	1			8		Water.	1	"	1,100
Schuylkill,			1	1840	Jefferson,	Schuylkill Haven,	David Potts,		M.	700		40	15	"	1			6½		"			800
	27	27	33							52,231	29,697	3,185	1,830										69,524

STATEMENT, showing the number and condition of each sort of **IRON WORKS**, and the capital invested in the Land and Buildings in each County in **EASTERN PENNSYLVANIA**, in the year 1850.

COUNTY.	ANTHRACITE BLAST FURNACES.						CHARCOAL BLAST FURNACES. HOT BLAST.					COLD BLAST.					BLOOMERIES.			FORGES.			ROLLING MILLS.			TOTAL.			Counties.
	S.* F.	†Un-fin'sd.	In.	Out.	Total.	Investment.	S.* F.	In.	Out.	Total No.	Investment.	S.* F.	In.	Out.	Total No.	Investment.	S.* F.	No.	Invest-ment.	S.* F.	No.	Investment.	S.* F.	No.	Investment	S.* F.	No.	Investment.	
1. Adams,					0					0				1	1	4,000		0			0			0			1	4,000	1.
2. Blair,					0		4	4	4	8	283,000		4		4	275,000		0		2	14	314,000		1	50,000	6	27	922,000	2.
3. Bedford,					0		1		2	2	25,000	1		1	1	10,000		0		2	3	18,000		0		4	6	53,000	3.
4. Berks,			1		1	65,000	2	4		4	201,000	1	6	2	8	335,000		0		5	23	320,000		5	310,000	8	41	1,231,000	4.
5. Bucks,		1	1		2	120,000				0					0			0			0			0			2	120,000	5.
6. Bradford,					0					0					0			0			0			0			0		6.
7. Carbon,	1		1	1	2	15,000		1	1	2	80,000				0			4	11,700		2	12,800		0		1	10	119,500	7.
8. Cumberland,					0		2	1	1	2	215,000	5		5	5	159,000		0		3	4	75,000		1	75,000	10	12	524,000	8.
9. Columbia,	5		5	6	11	745,000	2	2	2	4	51,000	1	1		1	3,500		0		1	1	5,000	1	3	303,000	10	20	1,107,500	9.
10. Chester,			1	2	3	300,000				0			2		2	200,000		0		1	6	106,000	2	14	642,200	3	25	1,248,200	10.
11. Centre,					0		1	1	1	2	180,000	5	4	4	8	308,000		0		2	5	63,000	2	5	114,000	10	20	665,000	11.
12. Clearfield,					0				1	1	84,000				0			0						0			1	84,000	12.
13. Clinton,					0		1	1	2	3	195,000	2		2	2	10,000		0			1	15,000		0		1	6	220,000	13.
14. Dauphin,	1			2	2	103,000	1	1	1	2	100,000	2	2		2	40,000		0			2	19,000	1	1	20,000	5	9	282,000	14.
15. Delaware,					0					0								0			0			1	16,000		1	16,000	15.
16. Franklin,					0		1	2		2	101,000	3	1	5	6	112,000		0		3	8	61,500	1	1	32,000	8	17	306,500	16.
17. Huntingdon,					0		6	6	3	9	345,000	4	3	3	6	230,000		0		5	11	256,000	1	2	65,000	16	28	896,000	17
18. Juniata,					0					0					0			0			0			0			0		18
19. Lehigh,			6	1	7	410,000			1	1	60,000	1		1	1	8,000		0			0			0		1	9	478,000	19.
20. Lycoming,					0		1		1	1	25,000		1	1	2	50,000		0			3	28,000		2	47,500	1	8	150,500	20.
21. Luzerne,			2	2	4	270,000		1		1	20,000				0			0			1	12,000	1	2	400,000	1	8	702,000	21.
22. Lebanon,		1	1	1	3	195,000				0			2	1	3	420,000		0			3	70,000		0			9	685,000	22.
23. Lancastèr,	3	1	5	3	9	305,000		3	2	5	335,000		1	1	2	95,000		0		2	12	223,000		2	315,000	5	30	1,273,000	23.
24. Mifflin,					0		3		4	4	95,000			1	1	10,000		0		2	2	60,000		0		5	7	165,000	24.
25. Monroe,					0					0					0			1	15,000		0			0			1	15,000	25.
26. Montgomery,	1		2	3	5	273,000				0				1	1	23,000		0		1	2	20,000		4	187,000	2	12	503,000	26.
27. Northumberland,	1		1	1	2	120,000				0		1		1	1	20,000		0			1	6,000		0		2	4	146,000	27.
28. Northampton,	1	1	2	1	4	260,000				0					0		1	1	2,000		0			1	35,000	2	6	297,000	28.
29. Potter,					0					0					0			0			0			0			0		29.
30. Perry,					0		2		3	3	90,000	1		2	2	30,000		0		1	1	60,000		1	185,000	4	7	365,000	30.
31. Pike,					0					0					0			0			0			0			0		31.
32. Philadelphia,					0					0					0			0			3	45,000	2	8	307,000	2	11	352,000	32.
33. Susquehanna,					0					0					0			0			0			0			0		33.
34. Sullivan,					0					0					0			0			0			0			0		34.
35. Schuylkill,	1	1	1		2	40,000		2		2	53,500			1	1	14,000		0		4	6	127,000	1	1	20,000	6	12	254,500	35.
36. Tioga,					0		1	1		1	20,000				0			0			0			1	5,000	1	2	25,000	36.
37. Union,					0		2	1	2	3	31,000				0			0		1	1	6,000		0		3	4	37,000	37.
38. Wayne,					0					0					0			0			0			0			0		38.
39. Wyoming,					0					0					0			0			0			0			0		39.
40. York,					0		2		5	5	278,000				0			0		1	3	90,000		0		3	8	368,000	40.
	14	5	29	23	57	3,221,000	32	31	36	67	2,867,500	27	27	33	60	2,356,500	1	6	28,700	36	118	2,012,300	12	56	3,128,700	120	364	13,614,700	

* Sold by the Sheriff, or failed, since 1840.

† On 2 of these furnaces the work has been suspended over a year. On 2 others the work will be completed, but they will not be blown in. The remaining furnace will be completed and blown in, as it is to take the place of another one worn out.

A Detailed Statement of all the ANTHRACITE BLAST FURNACES in the State of Pennsylvania, in the year 1850.

COUNTY.	Sold by Sheriff, or failed, and date.	No. Furnaces. Un-fin'd.	In Blast.	Out of Blast.	Date of construction.	NAME OF WORKS.	SITUATION. P. O.	OWNERS.	LESSEES.	* Kind of Ore used.	Largest Product. Tons.	Actual make 1849. Tons.	No. men and boys employed.	No. oxen, horses and mules employed.	BLAST. Heat.	Tuyeres. No.	Tuyeres. Diam.	Pres're.	STACK. Bos'h. feet.	Height. feet.	Kind of Power used, and No.	Kind of Metal made, and No.	Annual Capacity. Tons.
Berks,			1		1846	Henry Clay,	Reading,	Eckert & Bro.,	None.	H. M.	3,484	3,250	50	35	500°	3	3	3a4	14	37	Steam.	1	3,500
Bucks,		1	1		1848	Durham,	Durham,	Jos. Whitaker & Co.	"	"	3,840	3,840	103	32	500	3	3	3	13	40	"	2, 3	8,000
Columbia,	1843 S			1	1838†	Montour, 1	Danville,	Montour I. Co.	"	F.	3,135		70	5	612	3	2¾	4	9	31	"	3	3,150
do.	1844 S			1	1839	" 2	"	"	"	"	4,042		70	5	"	3	"	4½	12	33	"	3	4,100
do.	1844 S		1		1839	" 3	"	"	"	"	3,523	1,953	70	5	"	3	"	"	"	"	"	3	4,100
do.			1		1846	" 4	"	"	"	"	6,449	6,449	70	5	"	4	"	4⅝	14	34	"	3	6,500
do.	1842 S			1	1846	Franklin,	"	Jacob B. Maus & Co.	"	"	1,000	200	45	25	"	3	4	2	8	30	"	2, 3	2,000
do.	1848 F			1	1840	Roaring Creek,	"	Trustees U. S. Bank,	"	"	2,000		45	45	"	3	3	3	8½	32	Water.	1, 2	2,000
do.			1		1840	Columbia,	"	Geo. Patterson,	J. P. & J. Grove,	"	2,500	1,600	50	20	"	3	2½	5	8½	30	Steam.	1, 2	2,500
do.			2		1845	Iron Dale,	Bloomsburg,	Bloomsburg I. Co.	None.	"	10,200	8,132	180	80	550	3	3¾	2½	14	35	Water.	2, 3	10,200
do.				1	1845	Williamsburg,	Light Street,	M. McDowell,	"	"	1,200	800	40	25	500	3	3	1½	8	30	"	2, 3	2,000
do.				1	1847	Light Street,	"	Light Street I. Co.	"	"	1,000	550	40	20	"	3	2½	1¾	9	32	"	2, 3	2,000
Carbon,	1848 F		1		1838	Carbon,	Mauch Chunk,	J. Richards & Sons,	"	H. M.	1,500	1,500	53	8	"	3	3	3	8½	34	"	1, 2	2,000
do.				1	1826	Mauch Chunk,	"	Lehigh C. & N. Co.	"	"	4,052								8	28	"		2,000
Chester,				1	1845	Phœnix, 1	Phœnixville,	Reeves, Buck & Co.	"	"		1,534			612	3	3	4	12	38	Steam.	2, 3	4,100
do.			1		1845	" 2	"	"	"	"	3,910	3,910	371	114	612	3	3	4	12	"	"	2, 3	4,100
do.				1	1847	" 3	"	"	"	"	4,718	2,581			"	3	3	4	14	"	"	2, 3	5,000
Dauphin,				1	1845	Harrisburg,	Harrisburg,	D. R. Porter,	"	H.	3,614	3,360	71	48	"	3	3¼	3¾	12	35	"	1, 2	3,800
do.	1847 S			1	1834‡	Emeline,	Dauphin,	A. C. Bayard,	"	"	600		30	7	"	3	2⅝	2½	8	"	S & W.	"	2,000
Lehigh,				1	1840	Crane, 1	Catasauqua,	Lehigh Crane I. Co.	"	H. M.	3,958	3,639		300	"	3	3	4	11	45	Water.	"	4,000
do.			1		1842	" 2	"	"	"	"	4,833	4,494	500		"	4	"	"	13	"	"	"	5,000
do.			1		1846	" 3	"	"	"	"	7,144	6,139			"	6	"	"	17	"	Steam.	"	7,200
do.			1		1850	" 4	"	"	"	"					"	7	"	"	18	40	"	"	8,000
do.			1		1850	" 5	"	"	"	"					"	7	"	"	18	"	"	"	8,000
do.			1		1846	Allentown, 1	Allentown,	D. E. Wilson & Co.	"	"	5,000	4,200	200	250	"	3	2¾	2½a3	12	35	"	"	5,000
do.			1		1847	" 2	"	"	"	"	5,000	4,200			"	3	"	2½a3	12	35	"	"	5,000
Luzerne,				1	1842	Lackawanna, 1	Scrantonia,	Scrantons & Platt,	"	F. C.	1,800	1,800		225	450	3	2½	2	11	33	Water.	3	2,000
do.			1		1849	" 2	"	"	"	"	300	300	500		"	3	3½	2½	14	35	Steam.	3	3,500
do.			1		1849	" 3	"	"	"	"	300	300			"	3	3½	"	14	35	"	3	3,500
do.				1	1847	Jim Crack,	Wilkesbarre,	H. B. Renwick,	"	F.	1,300		50	20	"	3	2½	1	9	33	"	3	1,500
Lebanon,				1	1847	Lebanon, 1	Lebanon,	R. & G. D. Coleman,	"	M.	3,778	3,659	213	100	"	3	4	4	14	35	"	1, 2, 3	6,000
do.			1		1848	" 2	"	"	"	"	3,354	3,188			"	3	5	4	12	35	"	"	5,000
do.		1			1850	Cornwall,	Cornwall,	R. W. & W. Coleman,	"	"					"	3	4		12	38	"	"	5,000
Lancaster,			1		1848	Safe Harbor,	Safe Harbor,	Reeves, Abbott & Co.	"	H.	2,879	2,879	100	34	"	6	3¼	3¾	14	45	"	3	5,000
do.	1849 S			1	1844	Shawnee,	Columbia,	Wright & Nephew,	"	"	1,000		28	60	"	2	4		8	28	"	1, 2	2,000
do.	1849 S		1		1848	Cordelia,	"	Bryan & Longnecker,	"	"	700	250	28	71	612	3	3		8½	31	"	"	2,000
do.	1842 S			1	1841§	Sarah Ann,	"	Jno. B. Hertzler,	D. R. Porter,	"	1,664	200	24	30	"	3	3	3¼	8	30	"	"	2,000
do.			1		1845	Henry Clay,	"	Jno. Haldeman,	None.	"	2,678	2,159	50	36	"	3	3½	2¾	9	35	"	"	2,800
do.			1		1846	Chickiswalungo,	"	E. Haldeman & Co.	"	"	2,464	1,500	45	40	"	3	3	2½	8	32	"	1, 2, 3	2,500
do.				1	1847	Donegal,	"	Eckert & Stein,	"	"	3,472	3,472	46	44	"	3	3	4	10	35	"	"	3,800
do.			1		1849	Marietta,	"	Shoenberger & Musselman,	"	"	3,763	3,763	58	45	"	3	3½	3½	10	33	"	"	3,800
do.		1			1850	"	"	"	"	"					"	3	"	"	10	33	"	"	3,800
Montgomery,			1		1845	Plymouth,	Conshohocken,	S. Colwell,	"	"	3,338	2,492	185	40	"	3	3	3	11	36	"	1, 2	3,350
do.			1		1848	Merion,	"	Colwell & Co.	"	"	3,174	3,174	120	40	"	3	3	3½	14	38	"	"	3,500
do.				1	1844	Spring Mill,	"	Est. Farr & Kunzi,	D. Reeves,	"	1,000		100	40	"	3	3	4	12	40	"	3, 4	4,000
do.				1	1850	Swede,	Philadelphia,	Potts & Jones,	None.	"			110	20	"	6	2½	4	14	42	"	1, 2	4,000
do.	1849 S			1	1845	Wm. Penn,	Conshohocken,	Hitner, Reeves & Co.	"	"	3,120	2,044	95	42	"	6	2¼	2½	13	33	"	"	3,500
Northumberland,			1		1846	Chulasky,	Chulasky,	S. R. Wood,	"	F.	4,000	3,500	65	50	"	3	4	3½	14	34	"	2, 3	4,500
do.	1846 S			1	1842	Shamokin,	Shamokin,	Claghorn, Richards & Co.	"	C. B. F.	1,380		40	25	"	3	3	4½	12	45	"	1, 2	3,500
Northampton,	1849 S		1		1842	S. Easton,	Easton,	Thomas & Mills,	"	H. M.	3,140	3,140	50	20	"	3	2¾	3½	11	37	Water.	"	3,500
do.				1	1844	Glendon, 1	"	Chas. Jackson, Jr.	"	"	3,978	3,978	200	90	500	3	3	3	10	45	"	1, 2, 3	4,000
do.			1		1845	" 2	"	"	"	"	6,253	4,469			"	4	"	"	12	45	"	"	6,300
do.		1			1850	" 3	"	"	"	"					"	5	"	"	12	35	Steam.	"	6,300
Schuylkill,	1849 S		1		1838	Pioneer,	Pottsville,	The Greenwood Co.	Patterson, Richards & Co.	H. C.	1,742	570	60	25	612	3	3	4	9	34	"	1	2,000
do.		1				St. Clair,	St. Clair,	Burd Patterson,	None.	C.					"	3			14	32	"	1, 2	3,500
	14	5	29	23							151,331	109,168	4,225	2,126									221,400

* In the column of Ores, H. signifies Brown Hematite; M., Magnetic; F., Fossiliferous Red Oxyde; C., Carbonate; B., Bog Ore.

† Altered from Charcoal 1839. ‡ Altered from Charcoal 1848. § Altered from Charcoal 1845.

A Detailed Statement of all the ROLLING MILLS IN EASTERN PENNSYLVANIA, in the year 1850.

COUNTY.	Sold by Sheriff, or failed.	Date of construction.	NAME OF WORKS.	SITUATION. POST OFFICE.	OWNERS.	No. Puddling Fur.	No. Heating Fur.	No. Train Rolls.	No. Nail Machines.	CONSUMED. Bituminous Coal. Bush.	Anthracite Coal. Tons.	Pig. Tons.	Bloom. Tons.	Scrap Tons.	Largest Product. Tons.	No Furnaces running, 1850. Puddling.	Heating.	No. of men and boys employed	No. oxen, horses and mules employed.	Description of Iron made.	Kind of Power used.	Actual make, 1849. Tons.	No. run out fires.	Market
Berks,*		1845	Bertolet's,	Reading,	M. A. & S. Bertolet & Co.	4	4	2			4,000	1,800	150	50	1,500	2	2	60	2	Sheets, Bars, Rods,	Steam.	500		E.
do.†		1836	Reading,	"	Reading Iron and Nail Co.	12	3	3	30		14,000	5,000	200	100	4,275	6	3	155	3	Bar, Rods, Nails, Band and Hoop,	"	2,100		"
do.		1848	Birdsboro,	Birdsboro,	E. & G. Brooke,	4	2	1	16		3,000	1,200	100	100	1,000	4	1	100	4	Nails,	Water.	1,000		"
do.		1846	Gibraltar,	Robeson Township,	H. A. Seyfert, McIlvaine & Co.		2	1			900		600		600		1	10	4	Boiler,	"	400		"
do.		1845	Pine,	Douglasville,	Joseph Bailey,		2	1		25,000			850		850		2	18	6	"	"	850		"
Blair,		1839	Portage,	Duncanville,	Royer, McNeal & Co.	4	4	3	18	115,000		1,700	100	50	1,500	4	2	50	18	Nails, Plate, Bar and Rod,	Steam.	1,000	1	E. & V
Centre,		1825	Bellefonte,	Bellefonte,	Valentines & Thomas,	1	2	3		25,000		500	600		1,000	1	1	16	18	Slit Rods, Bars and Axles,	Water.	1,000		E.
do.		1831	Milesburg,	Milesburg,	Irvin, McCoy & Co.	1	2	1		37,500		500		20	1,000	1	1	30	26	Slit Rods, Bar, Wire-Billets,	"	800		"
do.	1849 S	1846	Hecla,	Zion,	Boyd & Cummings,	2	1	1		20,000		500			400			16	12	Plate and Sheet,	Steam.			"
do.	1843 F	1829	Eagle,	Milesburg,	C. & J. Curtin,	1	1	1		17,500		500			750	1	1	10	6	Wire-Billet and Shovel Plate,	Water.	546		"
do.		1840	Howard,	Howard,	Irvin, Thomas & Co.	3	1	1		30,000		1,250			1,000	3	1	18	3	Slit Rods and Bars,	"	400		"
Chester,		1838	Triadelphia,	Coatesville,	James Yearsley & Bro.	1	4	2		30,000		150	450	20	550	1	2	20	4	Boiler and Flue Iron,	"	550		"
do.		1844	Pine Grove,	Oakhill,	Enos Pennock,		2	1		12,000			400		400		1	9	4	" "	"	340		"
do.	1848 S	1845	Pleasant Garden,	N. London X Roads,	Ellis P. Irwin,	1	2	1		18,000			600		600			16	4	" "	"			"
do.		1849	Summerfield,	Pottstown,	Christman & Bro.		2	1										10	10	" "	S.&W.			"
do.		1830	Chester Co.	Phœnixville,	Jaudons & Mason,	7	2	1	40		4,000	2,200	100	100	2,000	7	2	70	2	Nails,	Water.	1,800		"
do.		1836	W. Brandywine,	Coatesville,	S. Hatfield,		4	2		30,000			1,000		1,000		4	30	14	Boiler and Flue,	"	1,000		"
do.		first built 1790 rebuilt 1835	Phœnix,	Phœnixville,	Reeves, Buck & Co.	15	4	4			6,988	5,785			5,251			130	15	Bar and Sheet,	S.&W.			"
do.		1846	Phœnix Rail Mill,	"	"	25	6	2			20,656	12,105			9,442	13	3	307		R. R. Iron,	Steam.	5,463		"
do.		1837	Hibernia,	Wagontown,	Charles Brooke,		2	1		14,000	20		400		450		1	16		Boiler and Flue,	Water.			"
do.		1810	Brandywine,	Coatesville,	Mrs. R. W. Lukens,‡		2	1		21,000	50		944		944		2	17	4	" "	"	944		"
do.		1825	Laurel,	"	Hugh E. Steel,§	1	2	1		20,000	50		854		854		2	18	10	" "	"	854		"
do.		1847	Thorndale,	Downingtown,	J. & J. Forsythe & Sons,	2	4	1		35,000		200	725		725	1	4	32		" "	Steam.	725		"
do.	1849 F	1795	Rokeby,	Coatesville,	Mrs. A. Fisler,		3	1		50,000	50		875		875			22	10	" "	Water.	150		"
do.		1840	Caln,	"	Pennock's Heirs,	2	3	2		50,000	50	800	800		Angle 600 Boiler 800			42	4	" and Rod,	"			"
Columbia,		1846	Montour,	Danville,	Montour Iron Co.	30	8	2			19,466	9,807			7,357	30	8	250	8	Rails,	Steam.	1,943		"
do.		1847	Rough and Ready,	"	Hancock & Foley,	4	2	2		2,000	3,000	1,050		50	955	4	2	62	2	Bar, Rod,	"	955		"
do.	1848 S	1845	Danville,	"	S. P. Case, (Davis, lessee,)	3		2			1,081	803			725			28	1	Pud. Bar,	"			H.
Cumberland,‖		1831	Fairview,	Harrisburg,	J. Pratt & Son,	5	3	3	36	90,000		1,800	50		1,500	5	3	75	30	Bar, Rod, Nails,	Water.	1,500		E. & F
Dauphin,	1842 S	1836	Harrisburg,	Harrisburg,	J. Pratt & Son,		2	1		13,000	500		400	25	400		2	14	1	Boiler,	Steam.	400		E.
Delaware,		1808	Franklin,	Chester,	J. G. Johnson,		1	1			300		10		220		1	7	5	Spring Steel, 210, Sheet Iron, 10,	Water.	220		"
Franklin,	1842 F	1810	Montalto,	Montalto,	H. & H. Hughes,		4	2		5,000				40	340		4	150	30	Bar and Rods,	"	340	1	H.
Huntingdon,	1850 S	1847	Juniata,	Shaver's Creek,	Ed. F. Schoenberger,	1	3	1		15,000		200			150			19	1	Boiler, Sheet,	"	100	1	W.
do.		1838	"	Alexandria,	S. Hatfield & Son,	2	3	2		55,000		660			1,000	2	3	45	22	Boiler, Sheet, Bar,	"	1,000	1	E. H. V
Lancaster,		1848	Safe Harbor,	Safe Harbor,	Reeves, Abbott & Co.	24	6	2		175,000	5,996	7,805			5,567	16	4	375	20	Rails,	Steam.	5,567		E.
do.		1828	Colemanville,	Lancaster,	R. & G. D. Coleman,		4	2	12		1,000		1,059		1,500		4	50	21	Boiler and Flue, Bar and Slit Rod, Steel,	Water.	237 871 106		" E. & F E.
Luzerne,	1848 S	1842	Wyoming,	Wilkesbarre,	T. T. Paine,	12	10	5	20		6,500	3,800			3,000			250	10	Rails, Bar, Nails,	Steam.			"
do.		1844	Lackawanna,	Scrantonia,	Scranton & Platt,	24	7	4	22		14,000	10,000			7,000	16	6	250	75	Rails,	S.&W.	6,000		"
Lycoming,		1842	Heshbon,	Newberry,	Wm. McKinney,	1	1	1		17,500		125	300		400	1	1	7	2	Bars,	Water.	350		E. & F
do.		1842	Crescent,	Trout Run,	C. G. Heilman & Bros.	2	1	2	7	30,000		350		20	300	1	1	20	6	Bars and Nails,	"	300		H.
Montgomery,¶		1846	Pottsgrove,	Pottstown,	Henry Potts & Co.	3	4	2			3,000	400	863		1,500	1	2	30	14	Boiler and Rods,	Steam.	Boiler, 863		E.
do.		1846	Norristown,	Norristown,	Moore & Hooven,	10	3	3			6,100	3,250	50	150	2,775	10	3	125	3	Bars, Band and Nail Plates,	"	1,775 1,000		" "
do.		1830	Conshohocken,	Conshohocken,	Jas. Wood & Sons,	2	2	2			1,200	600	200		350	1	1	22	1	Imitation Russian Sheet,	Water.	279		"
do.		1790	Cheltenham,	Philadelphia,	Mrs. H. M. Rowland,**		3	1		25,000			600		600		1	25	14	Boiler and Flue,	"	300		"
Northampton,		1837	Lehigh,	S. Easton,	Rodenbaugh, Stewart & Co.		4	3	6		1,500		1,000	50	Wire 1,050		2	65		Wire,	"	900		"
Philadelphia,		1845	Kensington,	Kensington,	Jas. Rowland & Co.	10	3	3			5,000	2,500	250	250	2,500	10	3	75	4	Bars, Rods,	Steam.	2,500		"
do.		1840	"	"	Jos. Jobson & Co.		2	2			500		1,300		1,200		1	8	2	Saw Plates, Spring Steel,	"	600		"
do.		1845	Penn,	"	Robbins & Verree,		4	2			1,250		200	1,800	2,517		2	28	4	Bars, Boiler, Slit Rod, Spring Steel,	"	1,685		"
do.		1846	Treaty,	"	Leiberts & Wainwright,	5	3	2			3,000	1,750			1,400			75	2	Bars, Rails,	"			"
do.	1848 F	1846	Fairmount,	Spring Garden,	Thomas & Ogden,	7	2	3			7,000	3,416	787	180	3,876			105	4	Bar, Rod, Band,	"			"
do.		1848	Fountain Green,	"	Jas. S. Spencer,	2	2	2		7,000	300	350		50	300			20	6	Rod, Spikes,	"	300		"
do.	1842 S	1820	Flat Rock,	Manayunk,	M. B. Buckley & Son,	1	2	2		12,000	750	225	450		600	1	1	18	4	Boiler and Flue,	Water.	600		"
do.		1842	Oxford,	Frankford,	W. & H. Rowland,		2	1		10,000	1,000		400	400	700		2	10	4	Spring and Saw Steel,	Steam.	600		"
Perry,††		1838	Duncannon,	Duncannon,	Fisher, Morgan & Co.	10	5	5	45	120,000	3,000	4,000	50	300	3,000	10	3	200	25	Bar, Plate, Rod,	Water.	2,975		E. & I
Tioga,		Unfinished.	Blossburg,	Blossburg,	J. H. Gulick,	1	1	1												Bars,	Steam.			H.
Schuylkill,‡‡	1844 S	1839	Franklin,	Port Clinton,	John Raush,	2	1	1			1,500	440		150	450	1	1	18	7	Bars,	Water.	50		E. & I
	12					247	164	106	252	1,126,500	140,707	87,521	17,717	3,905	91,598	153	97	3,648	511			54,738	4	

Schall & Dewees, Norristown, 24

Total No. Nail Machines in Eastern Pennsylvania, 276

* No bars made last year nor this year. † No bars made for market since June, 1848, now making nails and gas tubes only. ‡ Gibbons & Huston, lessees. § Steel & Worth, lessees. ‖ Have sold no bars in the city since 1847. ¶ Made no bar iron since January, 1848. ** Rowland & Hunt, lessees. †† Have sold no bars or rods in the city since November, 1848. ‡‡ No bars made for city market since 1847.

HOT BLAST CHARCOAL FURNACES IN EASTERN PENNSYLVANIA, in the year 1850.

COUNTY.	Sold by Sheriff, or failed.	No. Furnaces. In Blast.	No. Furnaces. Out Blast.	Date of construction.	NAME OF WORKS.	SITUATION. POST OFFICE.	OWNERS.	LESSEES.	Kind of Ores used.	Largest Product. Tons.	Actual make in 1849. Tons	No. of men and boys employed.	No. oxen, horses and mules employed.	BLAST. Heat.	BLAST. Tuyeres No.	BLAST. Tuyeres Diam.	BLAST. P sure.	STACK. Bosh. feet.	STACK. Height. feet.	Kin Power used.	Kind of Metal made. No.	Market for sales.	Capacity. Tons.
Blair,	1849 S		1	1836	Elizabeth,	Frankstown,	Samuel Good & Co.		F.	1,000		100	25	Hot.	2			8½	32	W.&S.	3	W.	1,600
do.		1		1815	Springfield,	Springfield Furnace,	Royer & Co.		F. & H.	1,820	1,560	80	50	"	2			8	30	Water.	3	"	1,820
do.	1850 S		1	1846	Gap,	E. Freedom,	Ed. F. Shoenberger,		F. & H.	1,260	1,260	45	43	"	1	2½		8½	32	"	3	"	1,600
do.		1		1811	Alleghany,	Hollidaysburg,	Elias Baker,		H.	1,751	1,062	80	60	"	2	2½		9	32	"	1, 2, 3	"	1,800
do.		1		1846	Blair,	Collinsville,	H. McNeall,		F. & ½ H.	911	911	76	27	"	2	2½		8	36	Steam.	3	W. & H.	1,400
do.			1	1832	Elizabeth,	Antestown,	Martin Bell,		H.	883	554	50	20	"	2	2½		8½	34	Water.	3	W.	1,600
do.	1850 F	1		1805	Ætna,	Yellow Spring,	Spang, Keller & Co.		F. H.	1,000	1,000	100	38	"	1	2¼		8	31	"	3	"	1,400
do.	1850 F		1	1837	Canoe,	Williamsburg,	"		H.	1,180				"	2	2¼		8	31	Steam.	3	"	1,400
Bedford,	S		1	1800	Hopewell,	Hopewell,	McDowell, Benedict and others,		F.	500	300	50	20	"	1			7	32	Water.	3	E. & W.	1,000
do.			1	1846	Hanover,	McConnelsburg,	John Potts,		H.	300		50	25	"	2	2½		7	30	"		H.	1,000
Berks,	1842 F	1		1777	Reading,	Furnace,	H. P. Robeson & Co.		M.	2,200	1,800	100	80	"	2	2	1½	9	30	"	2, 3		2,200
do.		1		1846	Hampton,	Hampton,	E. & George Brooke,		M.	1,550	1,550	50	30	"	2	2¾	1	7½	30	"	2, 3		1,200
do.		1		1836	Alsace,	Reading,	Clymer, Kaufman & Co.		H.	850	450	40	40	"	1	2		7½	30	"	1, 2, 3		1,550
do.	1842 S	1		1820	Windsor,	Mohrsville,	Darrach & Jones,		H.	1,200	900	50	50	"	2	3		7½	30	"			1,2[illegible]0
Carbon,		1		1834	Maria,	Lehighton, 2 m.	Thos. M. Smith & Est. T. S. Richards,		H.	2,059	1,884	153	58	600°	1		3	8	30	"	1		2,060
do.			1	1837	Pennsville,	E. Penn,	S. Balliet & Co.		H.	780	624	61	55	500°	1	2¼		7	30	"	1		1,000
Cumberland,	1837 S	1		1770	Pine Grove,	Carlisle,	Wm. M. Watts,		H.	1,600	590	61	41	Warm	2	2½		8	33	"	1		1,600
do.	1849 S		1	1795	Holley,	Papertown,	Farmers and Mechanics Bank,		M. & H.	800	350	70	40	"	2	2½		8	33	"	2, 3		1,400
Columbia,	1848 S		1	1839	Liberty,	Mooresburg,	Trustees U. S. Bank,		F.	1,000		80	30	Hot.	2	2½		8	30	Steam.	1, 2		1,400
do.		1		1836	Esther,	Catawissa, 3½,	S. B. Deemer,		F.	1,600	900	60	50	"	2	2½		7½	30	Water.	2, 3		1,600
do.		1		1845	Penn,	Catawissa, ½,	Fincher & Thomas,		F.	854	854	70	60	"	2	3		7½	29	"	2, 3		1,200
do.	1849 S		1	1837	Briar Creek,	Berwick, 2,	Charles Kalbfus,		F.	680	275	30	15	"	2	2¼ & 2¾		7	27	"	2, 3		1,000
Centre,		1		1790	Centre,	Bolesberry,	Thompson, McCoy & Co.		H.	1,400	1,200	75	50	"	2	3		8	30	"	3		1,400
do.	1849 S		1	1826	Hecla,	Zion,	Boyd & Cummings,		H.	1,000		60	18	"	1	2½		8	30	"	3		1,400
Clearfield,			1	1815	Karthaus,*	K.,	P. A. Karthaus, Jr.		C.	1,820		120	20	400°	3	2½	2	12	45	"	3		2,000
Clinton,	1849 S	1		1830	Mill Hall,	Mill Hall,	Wharton, Morris & Co.		H.	1,360	1,360	70	45	Hot.	2	4		8½	28	"	2, 3		1,600
do.			1	1811	Washington,	Kittany,	John Henderson,	W. Morris & Co.	H.	1,100		70	45	"	1			8	30	"	2, 3		1,400
do.			1	1834	Farrandsville,*	Farrandsville,	John O. Stearns,		F.	1,100		70	25	"	2			10	45	"	2, 3		2,000
Dauphin,	1847 S		1	1830	Victoria,	Dauphin,	A. C. Bayard,		H.	2,200		90	80	"	2	2½ & 3		9	45	"	1, 2		2,200
do.		1		1837	Manada,	W. Hanover,	E. & C. B. Grubb,	Grubb & Kintzer.	M.	2,215	1,800	106	70	600°	2	2¼	1¾	8¼	32	"	3		2,215
Franklin,	1842 F	1		1805	Montalto,	Montalto,	H. & H. Hughes,		H.	1,000	1,000	150	30	Hot.	2	2½ a 3		9	33	"	2, 3		1,800
do.		1		1837	Caledonia,	Grafenburg, Adams Co.	Thaddeus Stevens,		H.	800	750	80	34	"	2	2 a 3		8	33	"			1,400
Huntingdon,	1849 S	1		1844	Monroe,	Pine Crove, Centre Co.	James Irvin,		H. & F.	900	900	60	30	"	2	2		9	33	"	1, 2, 3		1,800
do.	S	1		1838	Mill Creek,	Mill Creek,	Irvin, Green & Co.		H. & ⅓ F.	1,367	1,367	70	40	"	1	2¾		8	30	"	3	E. & W.	1,400
do.	S	1		1816	Union,	Spruce Cr.,	Wallace's Heirs,	G. W. Patton & Co.	H.	1,200	800	60	25	"	1	2½		8	30	"	2, 3	E. & W.	1,400
do.			1	1796	Huntingdon,	Warrior's Mark,	George K. Shoenberger,		H.	1,650	1,100	130	50	"	1	2½		8½	33	"	3	W.	1,650
do.		1		1839	Edward,	Vineyard Mills,	Samuel H. Bell,		F. & H.	960	575	50	36	"	2	2		8½	32	"	2, 3	W.	1,600
do.	S		1	1832	Winchester,	Orbisonia,	T. T. Cromwell,	J. Wigton & Co.	H.	500	500	40	30	"	1	2½		8	28	"	2, 3	W.	1,400
do.	S	1		1830	Rockhill,	"	Isett, Wighton & Co.		F. & H.	850	850	40	34	"	2	2½		8	30	"	3	E.	1,400
do.	S		1	1837	Chester,	"	Pennock's Heirs,		H.	500		80	24	"	2			9	45	S.&W.	2, 3	E.	1,800
do.		1		1849	Rough and Ready,	Coffee Run,	James Entricken,	Wigton & Moore.	F. & ½ H.	357	357	48	27	"	2	2½		9	32	Water.	3	E.	1,800
Lehigh,			1	1826	Lehigh,	N. Whitehall,	S. Balliet & Co.		H.	1,430	1,204	90	60	500°	1	2¾		7½	31	"	1		1,200
Lycoming,	1843 S		1	1837	Ralston,	Ralston,	Lycoming Valley Iron Co.		C.	1,000		44	37	600°	3	3¼		10	35	"	2		2,000
Luzerne,		1		1846	Shickshinny,	Shickshinny,	Wilson & Koons,		F.	1,600	1,600	62	24	Hot.	2	2		9	30	"	1, 2		1,800
Lancaster,		1		1756	Elizabeth,	Brickerville,	R. & G. D. Coleman,		M.	1,900	1,500	60	50	460°	2	1½	1	9	29	S.&W.	1, 2, 3		1,900
do.		1	1	1832	Rock,†	Peningtonville,	Charles Brooks, Jr., & Co.		H.	1,156	1,051	100	90	"	2	2	1½	8½	29	"	1, 2, 3		1,200
do.			1	1800	Mount Vernon,	Elizabethtown,	E. & C. B. Grubb,		M.	1,300		100	30		2	2¼		8	32	"	2, 3		1,400
do.		1		1809	Conowingo,	Buck,	James M. Hopkins,		H.	1,300	870	100	75	212°	1	3		7½	30	"	1, 2		1,200
Mifflin,			1	1846	Isabella,	Lewistown,	A. B. Long,		F. & H.	1,300		55	40	Hot.	2	2¾		9	30	"	1, 2	E.	1,800
do.	S		1	1810	Hope,	Lewistown, 6 m.	D. W. Hewling,		F. & H.	1,000	1,000	55	30	"	2	2½		8½	31	"			1,600
do.	1849 S		1	1838	Brookland,	Waynesburg,	H. N. Burroughs,		H.	1,200		100	40	"	2	3		8	32	"	2, 3	E.	1,400
do.	1847 F		1	1838	Matilda,	Jackstown P. O. Huntingd'n Co.	J. F. Cottrell,		F.	1,200	800	60	30	"	2	2½		8	33	Steam.	1, 2	E.	1,400
Perry,	1847 S		1	1840	Perry,‡	Bloomfield,	Loy, Everhart & Co.		F. & H.	500		40	35	"	1			7		Water.	1, 2		1,000
do.	1849 S		1	1808	Juniata,	Newport, 3 m.	Cathcart & Co.		F. & H.	800	400	50	30	"	2			8		"	1, 2		1,400
do.			1	1836	Montebello,	Duncannon,	Fisher, Morgan & Co.		F.	1,449	1,185	70	35	"	2	1½		8½	32	"	2, 3		1,600
Schuylkill,		1		1830	Swatara,§	Pine Grove, 6 m.	Eckert & Guilford,		M.	1,880	1,300	103	33	Cold.	2	2¼		9	32	"	1, 2		1,880
do.		1		1835	Stanhope,	Pine Grove, 2 m.	W. S. & J. R. Breitenbach,		H.	788	788	65	38	Hot.	1	2¼		7½	30	"	1, 2		1,200
Tioga,	1849 F	1		1841	Blossburg,	Blossburg,	James H. Gulick,		F. C. B.	700	700	40	16	400°	1	4		7½	31	"	1, 2		1,200
Union,	S		1	1827	Berlin,	Hartleytown, 4 m.	C. & C. Brooke,		F.	900		60	30	Hot.	2			8	31	"	2, 3		1,400
do.	1848 S		1	1846	Forest,	Milton, 6 m.	Kaufman, Reber & Co.		F.	700		36	20	"	2			9	30	"	1, 2		1,800
do.		1		1848	Beaver,	Middleburg,	Middleswarth, Kerns & Co.		F.	1,200	1,200	50	36	"	2	2¾		8½	30	"	1, 2		1,600
York,	1842 S		1	1823	Margaretta,	Margaretta,	Hahn & Himes,	Curran, Himes & Co.	H.	1,100	745	100	30	"	2	2 & 3		7	32	Steam.	1, 2		1,200
do.			1	1827	Manor,	Chanceford,	John Herr,		H.	1,000	100	80	40	"	1	2		8	32	Water.	1, 2		1,400
do.			1	1830	York,	Chanceford,	John Bair,		H.	1,000	700	80	30	"	2	2½		9	32	"	1, 2		1,800
do.			1	1836	Codorus,	Manchester,	E. & C. B. Grubb,		H.	2,400	1,900	100	30	"	2	3		8	32	"	1, 2		1,400
do.	1842 S		1	1842	Woodstock,	Margaretta,	Hahn & Himes.	Curran, Himes & Co.	H.	1,000		75	20	"	2			10	40	"			2,000
	32	31	36							77,860	46,336	4,694	2,499										101,475

* Built for a Coke Furnace. † Now running Cold Blast. ‡ Abandoned. § Blast now running Cold, have a Hot.

www.ingramcontent.com/pod-product-compliance
Lightning Source LLC
LaVergne TN
LVHW021408110826
845150LV00007B/1839